DATE DUE

NOV 2 8 1990			

170 IDEAL   PRINTED IN U.S.A.

THE PASTOR
AND
HIS PEOPLE

THE PASTOR AND HIS PEOPLE

A Psychology for Parish Work

BY EDGAR N. JACKSON

INTRODUCTION BY JAMES A. KNIGHT, M. D., B. D.

CHANNEL PRESS, INC., MANHASSET, NEW YORK

CONTENTS

ACKNOWLEDGMENTS

Many people have helped to bring this book to completion. I am indebted to Professor L. Harold DeWolf for the critical reading of the chapter on theology, and for helpful suggestions on the general plan of the book.

Dr. Leonard S. Cottrell, Jr., a social psychologist; Dr. James A. Knight, a professor of psychiatry; and Dr. Walter Muelder, dean of a theological seminary, have given helpful readings of the manuscript and contributed both to its general plan and its specific details. In thanking them I express extra appreciation to Dr. Knight for writing the introduction. Also Simon Doniger has permitted use of material which first appeared in *Pastoral Psychology*.

All case material has been modified to make it impossible to identify the people involved. Case material is used only to the extent that it illuminates the problem at hand.

Much of the material in the book was first presented in lecture form to a number of seminaries and pastors' schools. Thanks go to those who made useful comments and critical evaluation. Most of all I acknowledge the contributions of thousands of parishioners who through thirty years of pastoral ministry have shared a valued and fruitful relationship.

EDGAR N. JACKSON

Mamaroneck, New York
January 2, 1963

INTRODUCTION

JAMES A. KNIGHT, M.D., B.D.

*T*HIS BOOK is addressed to the pastor. No professional person in our society has as great an opportunity for the prevention of emotional illness as does the parish minister. Also, in the disposition, referral, or early management of the mentally ill, he has the awesome distinction of having more

7

persons turn to him for help than members of any other profession, vocation or group in our society. This is well documented in the monumental report of the Joint Commission on Mental Health which reveals that forty-two per cent of people with emotional problems turn first to clergymen. Physicians in general see a much smaller percentage—twenty-nine per cent.

Thus, Dr. Jackson in addressing his book to the parish minister knows of the great challenges and frightening responsibilities imposed upon the pastor each day. This book deals with many practical aspects of parish life and shows how many of the insights of the present-day behavioral sciences are similar in concerns and goals to that of the New Testament tradition and borrows heavily from this ancient wisdom. The author knows well the language of theology and the behavioral sciences, and his synthesis of the resources of these two disciplines as they bear on pastoral work will be especially helpful to the pastor in the care and sustaining of his congregation.

The author gives a lucid interpretation of the medical profession's emphasis upon specializing in the treatment of parts instead of the whole patient and its dedication to scientific materialism. He points out that the antidote to this is beginning to come from a more wholesome understanding of man which is emerging from a new interest in medicine combined with an old emphasis on religion. The increased attention paid today to preventive medicine demands an approach to the whole man and not to a fragmentation. Comprehensive medicine has been forced to go beyond the organic and to consider also the psychological, social, and spiritual worlds of the patient. Dr. Jackson is right in stressing that the old method of dividing diseases into organic and functional is no longer valid or understandable.

The author never blurs his identity as a pastor, though the pastor's roles are many. In his discussion of the pastoral care of the ill, he points out how the minister, especially in the hospital, often seeks a minor healing role with Aesculapius when he should actually be serving Hygeia. (Hygeia symbolizes the innate quality of wholeness that moves a being toward the realization of his nature as a health-endowed being; whereas Aesculapius represents healing through the medical arts of repairing damage and disordered functioning.) In a minister's rightful insistence on being a member of the hospital team, he often seems more intrigued with the tasks of other members of the team and before long begins to lose the image of the pastor, to blur his identity, and to function as a pseudo-psychiatrist or in some other capacity hardly recognizable as pastoral care. This is tragic because the good pastor, clear in his identity and confident in his pastoral role, is desperately needed as a member of this team, not only to minister to the patient but to minister also to the members of the hospital team.

Some ministers feel extremely inadequate as a part of the hospital team, while others relegate in their thinking insignificant roles to all other team members. Can it be said that one member of the team has a more important role in healing than another? The recognition of God as a source of all healing will help us keep our efforts in the proper perspective regardless of the disciplines we represent.

The author courageously challenges the pastor to look at his own motivation for entering and continuing in the ministry and points out how many have explored with professional help their own personal psychodynamics. Such a discussion not infrequently frightens clergymen. And some seminary deans feel that tampering with motivation may affect adversely the already declining enrollment in seminaries. I think, however, the reverse is true. In almost every known situation where ministers or theological students have searched for insight into their own motivation and needs, they have become happier and more effective pastors. This has been true also of members of other disciplines.

I am deeply impressed with the author's insistence that the insights of modern psychiatry, psychology and the other behavioral sciences be brought to bear in every aspect of the pastor's work whether it be counseling, group work, preaching, visitation of parishioners, teaching or in an examination of his own life.

He raises searching questions which concern every pastor and gives answers which are valid. Many of the categories dealt with, such as children, the aged, and shut-ins are also deep concerns of other groups in our society. Yet the church has the greatest opportunity for a special ministry because of its unique spiritual and social resources which minister to the needs of these people and play a major role in the prevention of both physical and emotional illness.

On a number of occasions, physicians in writing for a reprint of a published paper have requested that I send an extra copy "to give to my pastor." There are numerous topics in Dr. Jackson's book which the pastor and his personal physician, or physicians in his congregation, should be discussing together. Since this book will reach initially the hands of clergymen, it would be very worthwhile if they made this book available to the physicians and medical students in their congregations and then later followed through with informal meetings for exploration of the themes which are of mutual concern to both disciplines. This type of reaching out for the physician seems highly appropriate. And this practical book, dealing with parish life as it manifests itself both in human misery and beatitude is made in all seriousness, because at those points where Dr. Jackson deals with the hazards of the vocation of the ministry, I feel that he could just as well have been speaking of the hazards of the vocation of medicine. Also, the clergyman and the physican see many of the same people daily. Each discipline can add to the effectiveness of the other in the ministry of healing.

PREFACE:
A THEOLOGY FOR PARISH WORK

*I*N MOST SEMINARIES there is a department of practical theology. The implication might be that there is another type of theology which could be called impractical. Whether practical or impractical, the pastor's basic views on the great issues of theology are inseparably bound up with the way he interprets his ministry to people. Therefore, it is important at the beginning of this practical handbook to consider the premises upon which we build our structure of human relationships. Our concept of God, and our materia theologica not only have a bearing on everything we say or do—they make us what we are.

Our work with people inevitably gains flavor and quality from our concept of man. Our concept of man and his purpose cannot be separated from our idea of God and his will for man. Our understanding of the nature of Christ determines how we relate the will of God to the life of man. What we mean by salvation determines how we work to bring the resources of faith into the life of our people to overcome failures and make the inner being fruitful.

Some theological viewpoints limit or confound the processes of parish work. For example, an idea of God as so transcendent that his nature is always aloof and separated from man and his needs cannot help but influence the goals of the parish ministry. Or an idea of God as completely immanent invites man to an unending routine of self-contemplation that has no horizons; this leaves man frustrated by a preoccupation with himself as a creature devoid of cosmic relationships. Such extremes do not satisfy our complex needs, and fail to furnish adequate motivation for a fruitful parish ministry.

The New Testament invites us to develop and employ a "theology of relationship." Expressed in simple terms, a theology of relationship assumes that the dynamic quality of life is a process of achieving identities that sustain and move life toward true fulfillment. This theology is not concerned with static states of mind or with fixed and final states of being. It is not primarily concerned with the end of man. Rather, it aids man with his daily living, since this process is part of the goal and is the point where spiritual growth takes place.

A theology of relationship is built on the premise that what man does is important to God, just as the nature of God is the essential fact upon which man builds his concept of self, relationship and cosmology. Man is what he is because he is a God-endowed and a God-conscious creature. The relationship between creature and Creator has a dual nature; it involves an endowment, which is the potential, as well as an achievement, which is the actual.

This reciprocity has about it always an element of being and becoming, and the challenge to a man's nature is to accept the inheritance and fulfill the true dimensions of his nature. As he achieves the capacity to forgive, so he seeks to be forgiven. He seeks to enter into the inspiration of worship as he is able to accomplish right relations with his brothers. He craves merciful treatment as he is able to discipline within himself a merciful attitude toward others.

The theology of relationship is not remote from life. It neither makes God into an image that is put upon a pedestal, nor into a vacuous abstraction impotent to affect thought and action. Rather it is engaged in the day-to-day struggle to find discipline, meaning and purpose in the multiplicity of selves, the turmoil of human relations, and the encounter of man with the cosmic forces that surround his being.

The teaching of Jesus emphasizes the nature of God as

dynamic relationship by using such terms as spirit, light, power, and love to designate the divine nature. These abstract qualities become personal and purposeful in the lives of those who feel a kinship with the infinite and the eternal, for these are the ones who are aware of their "power to become sons of God."

In the Sermon on the Mount Jesus is concerned with right relations within the self, since the attitude a man has toward himself becomes the source of his action. We confuse issues if we consider action apart from attitude. So Jesus throws us back upon the basic emotions. A house of life built on false and shallow emotional foundations is bound to be destroyed by the emotional storms of life. Hate is the emotion from which murder grows. Lust is the feeling that desecrates the sacrament of sex. Guilt and grief and persecution become different things depending upon the emotional climate from which they emerge. The quality of spirit that keeps God's purpose in focus achieves the purity of heart that is the basis for right relationships within the self.

Most of the turmoil and confusion of life occur when the multiple emotions of life develop without any hierarchy of values. When one feeling is considered to be as good as another, the inner conflicts of feelings pull life apart. When the emotions of life are organized around a purpose large enough to demand that each emotion take its proper relationship to the others, the well-ordered, healthful integration of being develops.

Jesus helped troubled and confused persons to reorder the emotions of life, so that the potential for love could become the actual of love. Mary Magdalene was a person with intensity of feeling. But before she met Jesus the intensity of feeling was paramount and led to frustration and futility. Jesus helped her discipline her feelings, thereby giving her direction and purpose in living. Then the feelings that had been a liability became an asset. Inner power was engaged so that the integrity of being was realized. The woman at the well in Samaria had experienced a fragmentation of life and a disorganization of relationships because strong emotion was unrelated to worthy purpose. Jesus created the conditions within which her life could be brought into a finer focus; she became a different person and her relations with the community also were markedly changed.

When a young man with a large physical inheritance came to Jesus, confused by the relationship between what he was and what he possessed, Jesus made it clear that he had to achieve an inner mastery that would give him power over the material things of life rather than letting them have power over him. The oft-repeated statements about rich men and their wealth, and the relation of God and mammon, are clear appeals for adjustment within the self at the point where values are achieved.

When tradition made men aware of the conflicts of values, Jesus again made the clear distinctions essential to bringing the inner self into healthy cooperation with the best. The Jewish tradition had developed a variety of external codes that atrophied men's inner ability to create values. Their energy was absorbed in adherence, and their souls slowly sank into superficialities. Jesus pointed out that

17

the good could be a hazard to the best. The devotion of men to false or trivial values was most disorganizing of all, since it took the very spiritual resources that make men aware of God's will and perverted it to the acts and attitudes that denied God's will and nature. The paralysis of the value-creating center of being was the most inexcusable error of institutional religion.

Right relationship within the self is the essential for all other relationships. The ability of a man to value himself, even to love himself, is basic to self-fulfillment. This self love, however, is not a form of self-indulgence that leads to disintegration. Rather, it is a high self-regard that demands self-discipline.

What is true for the individual is also true for the structure of relationships we call group life. In church, school, business, political life, neighborhood activity, and family life, a projection of the self takes place that has a reciprocal quality. This self-projection is a dynamic thing, and is continually being modified just as it is at work to modify. What happens in the group is continually at work to shape the future responses of the individual. No one can live apart from the group, but no one can enjoy the relationships within the group unless he has a normal, healthy attitude toward himself and others.

Jesus pointed this out in the parables of the broken relationships. Meaning disappears and life is threatened when the structure of relationships that give life its meaning are broken. It does not make a difference whether the relationships are broken by chance, carelessness or design—the end effect is the same.

In the parable of the lost coin Jesus makes it look as if this accidental separation was a minor tragedy in the home where it happened. A coin that is not available for circulation, that is not a living symbol of value in the realm that gives it status, is nothing. It has its meaning only in its relationship. So the housewife called in her neighbors and they searched everywhere, sparing no energy, until the coin was found. When it was restored to its right relationship, its meaning was given back to it. So with the person who because of some accident gets separated from the social structure that gives his life meaning. It may be unemployment, an economic accident; or illness, a physical accident; or bereavement, an emotional accident, that has broken the fabric of human relations. When this happens, the concerned community is at work to overcome the accidental factors that have diverted life.

In the parable of the lost sheep Jesus shows how the sustaining relationships may be broken by carelessness. The lost sheep did not intend to wander away, but it became preoccupied with the green grass that was right under its nose. It lost sight of the group factors important for health and security. As with a business man giving all his thought to making money, or a society woman giving herself to a ridiculous ritual of entertainment, or a teacher absorbed in subject matter, or a hypochondriac absorbed in symptoms, the *larger* structure of life was lost.

When it was too late, the sheep realized it was lost, yet there was one person, symbolic of group concern, who overlooked personal hazard in order to restore the lost sheep to its group life. Only then was the sheep safe from the

19

dangers that would have destroyed it. The concerned community does not really care whether it is by accident or by carelessness that separation takes place. It is only interested in restoring the essential relationship so that life can function as it was intended.

In the parable of the lost son a different factor exists. The human has the capacity for free choice. He may choose the creative life or the destructive life. He may follow the way of resentment, anger and deliberate self-injury. He may run away, squander his resources, violate the confidences of those who love him, bring suffering and injury to family and friends. He may be unfaithful, intemperate, or irresponsible. He may turn his back on the values that were part of his life, and make it clear to those who feel loving concern that he wants none of their interest or their sympathy. He merely wants to be let alone so that he can go and do what he jolly well pleases. He takes his inheritance and in an act of defiance of the past throws it away on the very things he has been trained to avoid. A wise and good father encourages the development of freedom and choice; but what can the father do when the freedom is turned to destructive ends? He watches and waits, and he keeps on loving and praying. When he has a chance, he moves toward the separated one in love and affection to support every right feeling and overlook the errors that have marred the past. The important thing is that the one who was separated from the meaningful structure of relationships has come to himself and wants to reestablish himself in the framework of persons and values that he has turned his back on for a while.

Whether it be a relationship with things that gives useful direction to human energy, or with an organized group that guarantees protection and security, or a relationship to those who represent meaning and value in life, the important emphasis is always on restoration to the relatedness that gives meaning to life.

Jesus makes it clear that the self is fulfilled in the group, but also that for man as a social being the contribution of the group is essential to life as God plans it. Jesus even goes further and points out that community with God and the processes of proper worship are contingent upon achieving right relationships within the group. Sacramental acts are second to the acts of love and understanding between brothers.

This leads to the third level of relationships—one built on right relationships within the self and the group, but one which goes further in a bond of communication between creature and Creator. Jesus makes it clear that his relationship with God is an achievement. It is built on an acknowledged cause-effect process. "The spirit of the Lord is upon me because. . . ." In John he makes it clear that the Creative Being, the Word, is alive in him through a spiritual resonance that makes them one in fact though two in expression. "I and the Father am one." The compound subject has a singular verb and a singular predicate adjective. But he does not stop there. He says that this unity of being is not a unique achievement but is also a possibility for those who fulfill the demands of the relationship, and he predicts that they will not only do what he has been able to do but more also.

21

Jesus claims that it is the main purpose of his life to know and do the will of God. The preservation of life is secondary to this purpose. The strength of his life grows from his undivided loyalty to that will. The major discipline of his life is to seek that will through unending communication.

When Jesus examines the lives of persons about him, he sees the will of God being violated. This brings into life its frustration and suffering. Sometimes the innocent suffer, and sometimes the arrogant gloat over the power they have to violate and confound the will of God. Sometimes the will of God is violated by ignorance of what is God's plan and purpose for life. Men contend with God's will by imposing their own. Unaware of a larger plan for their existence, they engage in destructive acts and suffer the consequences of their ignorance. Often this ignorance is not limited to themselves but projected outward to cause suffering for others. Then the innocent suffer; the experience of the rejection of Christ's revelation stands as an example.

At other times men confound the will of God through carelessness. They fail to practice the good they know through indolence, laziness, and lack of concern. This has its effect upon the individual but it can also involve the innocent bystander. In the close-knit fabric of the community, the tragedy and suffering that grows from carelessness is an unending trial, and none escape some of the repercussions of it. Like ignorance, carelessness can fracture the sustaining relationships of life.

Men also use their freedom deliberately to do what they know is wrong. They injure and destroy themselves and knowingly injure and damage the lives of others. They resist the will of God by direct action or subtle evasion. They make trivial rites of the great affirmations of life. They give themselves to the letter of the law in place of its spirit. The people who invited the wrath of Jesus were those who escaped into the trivia of moral codes and traditional practices instead of showing true value for the welfare of their brother men. Jesus recognized the inclination toward ignorance and carelessness as a part of man's estimate of himself as a finite being struggling with an infinite value placed upon himself. He was less inclined to accept the acts of those who knew better but still chose the way of compromise and willful action when faced with the revelation of the will of God.

The theology of relationship is expressed in the efforts of Jesus to bring his followers to a level at which they could practice the truths about life he revealed. It is no mistake that these persons were called disciples, for they were the ones chosen to practice the discipline. The ultimate in right relationship was the quest for the will of God in the compounded relationships of life. Here was the struggle for discipline that brought a kingdom of love and understanding into the daily practice of living.

This theological emphasis was never separated from the tasks of life. The temptation to employ spiritual power in place of the cause-effect process was faced early in Jesus' ministry. Rather than resort to miraculous acts he gave his allegiance to the major miracle of existence, the fact that the finite and the infinite, the space bound and the boundless, the creatures and the Creator could achieve a life-enriching relationship. He saw the potential for this relationship everywhere about him. He saw his mission as the releasing of the self-imposed bonds upon life so that the divine inheritance of men could be realized. In his dealing with people this was always kept in focus.

In this process of finding God's will for life, being and becoming were never separated. Becoming was a dynamic of life that involved expectancy, growth and disciplined achievement. Jesus pointed to the growing edge of the life of a child and set it as a model. The child is not afraid to ask and receive. The child bristles with curiosity about meanings, expectancy about relationships and an unself-conscious acceptance of the innate qualities of his becoming. He does not resist or resent growth. He cooperates with the plan and pattern of God for his life as revealed through the process of growth. The same qualities carried on throughout life make it possible for spiritual growth to move man closer to the way of life God seeks for man and reveals through Christ.

But the process of spiritual emergence is interfered with. As in the life of the child there comes a time when hesitant and doubt-filled questions are asked, so the adult hesitates to ask or receive because he becomes aware of the fact that every receiving has an obligation. To ask for and receive the revelation of God restricts life at the same time that it sets it free. Like the ambivalence of love, the privileges granted place restraints on life. We would seek the privileges, but become restive under the restraints, for part of our nature is not easily tamed and brought under the control of the highest will we can know.

So man is caught in the grip of failure when he is within sight of success. He feels bound by impulses that he does not easily tame at the same time that he is most anxious to set his spiritual nature free to achieve life's richest meaning. He knows that in himself he is a creature of space, time, habits, impulses, and death, yet he would dwell amidst the things of the spirit, of light and power and love. If he is to succeed at all in his struggle for values, he must relate himself to something beyond himself that strengthens his spirit and becomes a perpetual source of guidance and strength. Only then can he begin to be the person God has made it possible for him to be.

Here then he makes a great choice that leads to a great dedication. He tries to keep from standing in the way of God's will for his life. He seeks a rebirth wherein the impulses for growth are set free in him. This second birth is a realization of spiritual necessity but it is also a reorganization of life so that the elements of being are marshalled under the authority of the spiritual nature as revealed through Christ. His whole being then becomes a process of practicing the will of God as he finds it revealed through the indwelling of the Holy Spirit. In this process of spiritual self-discipline he finds the will of God as the primary guide for living. The lesser and contending elements of his nature are then reorganized about a purpose so compelling that the total resources of being are dedicated to life's more abundant revelation.

Although man may not understand all of the factors involved in the reintegration of his nature about the power of the indwelling spirit, he is never merely an interested bystander watching his life being manipulated by mysterious forces he cannot understand or control. He is part of the process, and in the achievement of this inner unity of being with high purpose, he is a major contributive factor. As his lungs are made for air, and his eyes for sight, so his soul is made for God. While he did not make his lungs or eyes or soul, he has much to do with the process by which they are used for the purposes God has set.

The impact of this upon life becomes everywhere evident. It is God-endowed life at work to realize the full potential of the endowment. Seeing is a learned response of most intricate design. The Yogi tells us that breathing is a fine art learned with long practice and exacting discipline. So also the development of the spiritual resources of life demand practice and discipline. Here the leader of the spiritual community achieves his function as guide, teacher, counselor as well as a source of inspiration. He is engaged in a way of life that communicates a way of life.

A theology of relationship seeks to make man aware of his relationship to God so that all of life shows the results of this awareness of God's will. Because it is centered on process and relationship there is no part of life that is beyond its reach. It is never remote and abstract, but always as near as the next person and as real as the next breath of air. So a theology of relationship is inevitably relevant. The necessity for making the ministry relevant depends upon recognizing the relevance of theology for all of life.

Let us look, then, at the practical applications of this theological emphasis on relationship.

In a democracy men's minds are challenged by the claim

of freedom and the obligation of mutual trust. The practice of democratic trust is involved just as much in the day-to-day process as it is in the ultimate goal. In fact, the ultimate goal has no prospect or relevance apart from the skills and disciplines of right relationship. The burden of political activity, as well as the development of good will in international acts, is never separated from the working out of God's will among men. Democracy guarantees men's right to make mistakes and experience failure as a necessary foundation upon which freedom of choice can be practiced. Here men can learn the trust and good will that modify carelessness and overcome ignorance. Democracy also makes it possible for men of ill will to practice wilfullness, thereby forcing upon the community the necessity for contending with the abuse of freedom through understanding and a more demanding concept of good will. Here the ethics of the second mile are applied; only as some men are willing to do more than is expected of them can the foundations of right relation with freedom be made secure. This concept has a relevance for life as everpresent as the newspaper headlines in this morning's press.

In education one generation seeks to pass on to another its experience, insight, and discipline. When the process is bogged down in subject matter, it loses sight of the relationships that make education desirable. The being whose life is led out through the processes of instruction is dynamic, and always more than the accumulation of the facts he knows or the routines he has mastered. Only when the educational process is tinctured with a major concern for the values of life and the uses of freedom will what is

learned be given its larger relevance. A theology of relationship is as relevant for life as a bulging bus on its way to
school, or a child meandering across lots to the one-roomed
building where the law demands his presence.

What is true of education is even more relevant in
learning the fine art that brings persons together in love
and shared responsibility. A theology that makes sex sin-
ful is ignoring the most powerful form of human communication. Here the sacredness of being can be developed
through the sacramental use of a force designed to bring
persons together in order to find the fulfillment that cannot
be achieved in any other way. The problems and privileges
of marriage and family life are rooted in relationships that
can warp and destroy as well as become beauty-filled. A
theology of relationship that teaches mutual respect and
shared realization in harmony with God's wisdom in creating men, women, and children is as relevant as a newborn
babe and far more hopeful than a divorce court. A shared
growth in understanding the mutuality of a life of love may
be a difficult and at times painful achievement, but it fulfills a basic design of creation as it brings humans to the
place where they stand as partners of God in the creation
of a soul that is capable of standing before God in awe and
reverence.

One does not begin to understand the meaning of the
church as an institution until he sees it not as an end but
as a means to an end. Within it the group life can be culti-
vated so that in mutual concern people may practice the
virtues of patience, understanding and good will. Here in
the safety of the understanding group the injured person

may be able to express the feelings he cannot express else-where. The church may become a microcosm of group living within which the processes of experimental living can be moved forward, and the disciplines of practical brotherhood be realized. Within the freedom of the institution the practice of sacramental silence among the Quakers on the one hand may share the meaning of high churchmanship on the other as a quest for the ways men grow in understanding of themselves and the relationships that enmesh them. It becomes a travesty of values when the religious institution is used to create intolerance and ill will. The church truly becomes the church only when it is the means of helping men understand and accept themselves and others as they grow in their awareness of the Nature of God.

Even the thorny problem of the mind-body relationship that is the focal point of psychosomatic study becomes a relevant theological interest when it is understood that illness is a type of organic behavior. This behavior is an expression of conflict and stress within the organism, and the symptoms that are the expression of it may well be the concern of medical science, but the roots of the organic activity as a struggle for relationship with self, others, and ultimate meaning remain the material of religious inquiry. Faith is then seen as the ultimate source of true wholeness of being, and the healing power of integrating trust is not to be discounted. The practices of religion and the processes of psychological organization take on a new relevance when illness is interpreted as behavior and health is understood as a way of life that has found adequate meaning consciously, as well as unconsciously. More than we are aware, the true source of illness may lurk behind such questions as "What can give my life meaning?" or "What is the matter with you?" or "Why can't I find inner peace?" Here the theology of relationship has a special relevance.

The church has a ministry to the sick and the well, not primarily in justifying failure and rewarding the symptoms of it, but rather by holding an ideal of human perfectability, and emphasizing the importance of individual effort in achieving it. The nature of sin, then, is not so much an act against God as an act against the God-created self and the sacred community within which the God-endowed self is seeking to work out its ideal of perfectability. "Be ye perfect as your Father in Heaven is perfect." The concern is with the inner kingdom which is the primary responsibility of each individual. God is not on the defensive, for God is beyond the defenses of man; but God is involved in the offenses of man, as the Cross so clearly reveals. Man's failures must not be conceived of primarily as a signal for cosmic retribution, but rather as the invitation to share that divine grace which helps us learn from failure and grow through it to the fruits of grace. The nature of God is forgiving love, not vengeful punishment. As Jesus pointed out, if a human father knows how to do good for his children, how absurd it would be to think of the Creative Being, whose nature is love, resorting to the total destruction of what he had made in wrathful punishment. Rather, with infinite patience and love he gives new opportunity for growth and spiritual understanding, even to that lost moment when man may glimpse a far horizon, long obscured, and hear the words,

30

"This day thou shalt be with me in paradise." Salvation then is more concerned with restoration than with judgment, and the instruments that work for salvation cannot be bound to small codes and judgmental practices without obscuring the nature of God they would reveal.

In this practical approach to a theology for the parish ministry, the working relationship takes on an exalted status, for it is engaged in the creative process that is the important achievement of life. All that is done becomes important, whether it be the routine of work or home or the deliberations in the committees of a church or social agency. The processes of understanding and good will, and the practice of spiritual growth in the important engagements of life is the very stuff of which God's kingdom is being built. Here is where any final triumph of righteousness will come, for the individual self with its efforts—and the selves at work in a group with their common efforts—become the focal point of spiritual growth.

Inevitably there are psychological aspects of theology just as there are theological implications in any psychological insight. But life can never get started on the road to achievement unless it achieves a meaning and purpose for the processes in which it is participating. The supreme relationship is found at the point where life finds its most abundant meaning. Theology in that light is not so much a study as it is a resource for spiritual realization.

Then the traditional elements for the theological structure take on new meaning and relevance for the work of the minister in the parish. The place of man in his own sight and in the plan of God becomes the starting point in the adventure of finding life's finest meaning. The nature of God is explored with enthusiasm, since this is the cosmic counterpart of man's spiritual awareness and it is actively engaged in aiding man as he moves toward the abundant life as man is in his own behalf. The revelation of Jesus, the Christ, becomes the bridge that relates creature and Creator in the forms of communication that bring the quest within the bounds of realization. The moral nature find its meaning in this relationship between the human searching and the divine disclosure in the practical terms of living. The social nature of man is the framework within which the practice of spiritual living takes place, and the church is the effort to create a spiritual institution that aids in the practice.

The ultimate end of man, then, is not remote from God but is immersed in the nature of God. The trinity becomes a living symbol of the relationships that theology affirms, with the first person representing the cosmic impulse toward disclosure of the spiritual nature of life, the second person as the living revelation of that relationship, and the third person representing the individualized and disciplined expression of God's will in the life of the person who gives himself without restraint to achieving the relationship between man and God.

If we would make the ministry relevant, we would start and end with theological assumptions that are relevant. The structure of relationships revealed in New Testament teaching and practice give the foundation for a parish ministry close to people and close to life because at no point is the work of the ministry conceivably separated from the quest for the will of God in the affairs of men.

THE PASTOR
AND
HIS PEOPLE

1

THE PASTOR'S CARE OF HIMSELF

*T*HE FIRST PERSON any pastor must deal with is himself. He must use the resources of his body, mind and spirit in the work of the ministry. He can never get away from himself. His strengths and weaknesses show up in every encounter. And so his management of his own inner life has a direct bearing upon those many relationships that bind him to others as pastor, preacher, and counselor.

Yet it is a disconcerting fact that often the basic emotional needs of the pastor are neglected in the variety of concerns that surround his call to the ministry, his preparation for it, and his practice of it. Does anyone ask about the deep emotional drives that send a man into the ministry? Is any consideration given to the emotional needs that persist in his professional activity? Is any help given him in resolving those emotional problems that complicate his parish ministry and produce unhappiness for himself or for those among whom he works? Let us illustrate the problem.

John W. has been serving parishes for more than thirty years. The word "parishes" is plural with a vengeance. He has served seventeen in the thirty-one years since his ordination. John is a man with talent, an adequate formal training and a pleasing personality. He makes a good first impression in all his parishes; but invariably, before six months have passed, he has begun to run roughshod over the feelings and opinions of other people. He sets group against group and turns the congregation into warring camps. Ultimately he is likely to seek out his superior with a request for a transfer because of "a certain group that is hard to deal with." Sometimes, however, the church members take the lead and request a change "for the good of the parish." John is on the defensive, many parishes have been injured, and many people disillusioned. Nevertheless, no one has taken any interest in the basic problem, which is John and his unresolved reservoir of aggressiveness. A potentially useful life is being wasted because he has not been helped to deal with a troublesome part of his own nature.

A different set of emotions was at work in Leslie J. He, too, was adequately trained, had a good cultural background, gave himself without reserve to the tasks of the ministry as he saw them, yet never seemed to accomplish anything really important. He became so enslaved by the trivial demands of the parish that he was uninspiring and uninspired when opportunities for leadership arose. He was always available for free taxi service, and he spent many hours doing household chores for elderly ladies in the parish. He shoveled snow, mowed lawns and raked leaves. He gave of himself freely, but without discrimination, and won the reputation of being too good to people. What most people did not understand was that Leslie J. had an overwhelming feeling of guilt deeply rooted in his childhood. He felt that he had to prove himself to his parents or anyone who filled a parent's role in his life. His energy was consumed in trying to prove something no one was asking him to prove. He was dominated by an unresolved emotional need.

Fred K. was a brilliant man. He had an excellent record in seminary, was an unusually capable speaker and had strong leadership abilities. He appeared destined for a fine, satisfying, and productive ministry. But what happened? He went from growing parish to growing parish doing effective work in most of the ways that could be observed. But there was a large blank spot. He could not go near sick people. He could not enter a hospital. He became ill at the variety of odors associated with a hospital or sickroom. He tried to force himself to do all this, but his discomfort was so intense that he did more harm than good. Sometimes he would drive around the hospital for an hour and then head away in defeat. No one ever made a serious effort to help Fred resolve his deep emotional problem, and he finally resigned from the parish ministry to take an administrative post in the church.

William L. was a dynamic individual, always willing to debate any issue, an able administrator, and a forceful speaker. His unbounded energy kept him engaged in numerous projects. The nature and purpose of the project seemed to be secondary to a compelling need to burn up the energy of his life. He had a deep problem that could not be dealt with therapeutically in the pastoral ministry. He could not be around women without being overcome with inappropriate urges. Such a compulsive attitude was a source of anguish to a morally rigid man, and obviously a threat to his ministry. He finally retreated into an office job, where his contacts with the opposite sex were at a minimum. A therapeutic approach to his compulsion early in his ministry undoubtedly would have changed the course of his life. It would have increased his competence in working with people and would have pacified his perpetually troubled soul.

In each of these instances, a man of considerable ability led a tortured existence and was prevented from realizing full effectiveness in his ministry because he was unaware of the nature of the problem that distressed him.

These are unusual cases, to be sure, and point to the need for help from a therapist. More prevalent are the problems that ministers share with most people in a harried world: discouragement that one's goals in life seem out of reach, disillusionment over a joyless marriage and unhappy children, lack of time to enrich the mind and spirit, fatigue and helplessness under the burden of other people's troubles.

The pastor's principal problem is the one most easily stated: He is expected to practice what he preaches. His people want to be able to think of him as a model of mental and physical health, a fount of wisdom and sound judgment, a disciplined spirit with impeccable moral standards, an encyclopedia of information. Aware that this is the image to which they want him to conform, he is also aware of his weaknesses; thus he is in constant anxiety, since he knows that his life is an open book to his people. If he fails to conquer or control a flaw in his personality or character, the result will be more than disillusionment on the part of his followers. The great cause he represents will suffer.

His dilemma may be stated in another way. He is involved in the predicament of man at the same time that he is seeking the solution to that predicament. If he is to "save" others, he must first "save" himself. If he is to heal others, he must first heal himself. If he is to lead others to the abundant life Christ promised, he must first find it himself.

The first step toward resolving that dilemma must be a vigorous, divinely-inspired self-interest—not selfish preoccupation leading to self-indulgence and dissolution of discipline, but serious concern for oneself as a creature endowed by God to attain spiritual maturity. That kind of self-interest leads to discipline, self-regard, and fulfillment.

While there are many selves struggling for recognition within the personality, we will refer here to only four: the body-self, the mind-self, the spirit-self and the social-self.

The noble image of a man propelled by the spirit of God can be ignobly shattered by such superficialities as excessive eating, visible fatigue, stooped shoulders, a dragging step and, above all, a querulous recital of ailments. Thus the pastoral ministry to the sick makes it important for the spiritual guide to have a healthy and robust body.We know that his mind and spirit are reflected in the condition of his body, but there are also practical disciplines he must master: wise and temperate eating habits, regular exercise, sufficient rest, good posture.

The discipline of the mind follows a similar pattern. The formal training of a professional person helps him to develop thinking habits useful in his major activities, but it may also limit his interests. It is certainly no guarantee of continuing intellectual stimulation. No minister is worthy of his calling if he allows his mind to atrophy through lack of mental exercise.

The vitality of the mind can be gauged in part by the material it ingests. A bishop was heard to remark, "When I look at the bookshelves in a minister's study, I can tell in what year his mind died."

But the variety and intensity of a man's mental life can also be measured by the music he listens to, the lectures he attends, and the television he watches. Only if the doors of his mind are open can he be aware of the cosmic dimensions of life.

The healthy body and growing mind are essential to the welfare of all men, but the development of the spirit-self is first in importance to the spiritual leader. And how easily he may neglect his own spiritual life!

This spirit-self is not demanding. It is so quiet that its needs can be muffled by the clamor of life's minor exigencies. It waits in silence for recognition and nourishment. Yet the spirit of man is the candle of the Lord. Its light is the spark that can penetrate the darkness and give life meaning.

We are assured that God speaks to us not in the loud or earth-shaking events, but in the "still small voice." The conditions for hearing that voice require the severest discipline of all: the cultivation of the quietness that leads to meditation, contemplation, prayer. An Indian student recently remarked, "In your country when you pray, you talk. In my country when we pray, we listen."

Often we deny ourselves the benefits of spiritual insight because we do not prepare ourselves to receive them. The pastor who neglects the springs of the spirit may travel for a while on the momentum of his "first fine careless rapture," but his inspiration will eventually wear thin and his soul will suffer. Each man needs his own equivalent of the desert place where he can go apart for a while to listen, to receive, to communicate with the divine source of truth and power.

Perhaps the self that stirs up the greatest conflict is the

social self. The pastor represents a religious judgment upon the community at the same time that he is obliged to participate in its social, religious, political, educational, and recreational activities. If his judgments are too harsh, he sets himself apart. If his judgments are not sharp and clear, he loses his chance to represent values toward which the community could move.

A pastor so rigid in his attitude toward minor foibles that he cannot see the deep problems of people is separating himself from life. The privilege of leadership is equally compromised by the "good Joe" with his indiscriminate participation in questionable practices and attitudes.

The pastor must be aware of the emotional significance of his social behavior. If he loudly affirms that "no one can tell *me* not to smoke or drink," he is showing a thinly veiled aggression against authority that threatens the values involved in his total ministry. When he slyly tells biological jokes or swears occasionally with self-conscious daring, he is announcing that he is not a typical, strait-laced minister. His emotions in such situations are more significant than the resultant behavior and he should probe them with thoroughness and care. When a man is not secure in his conviction, he may resort to actions and attitudes that divert him from his important goals. He must balance his inner conviction with an understanding of the nature of his people to produce a quality of human relations that will help him continually grow in favor with both God and man.

Only the pastor can evaluate himself when his emotional life is confounding his ministry. Except in extreme cases no one else will do it for him. Yet this candid look at the self is difficult and painful. The more painful it is, the more subtle are the escapes and the more formidable the defenses that the personality erects around its sore spots.

A familiar defense is to blame others for what has gone wrong. One can quickly determine a man's emotional temperature by listening to what he has to say about his parish members, especially the officials. If they are "stupid, unimaginative, antagonistic, and resistive of wise leadership," the pastor reveals his own inability to understand and work with those who may differ with him. Or he may blame his family background, or improper training, or even his wife for the events that have made his ministry less than satisfactory. Unreasonable criticism of others is a mirror that reflects the inner state of being.

Retreat into ill health, with its guarantee of sympathy, relief from responsibility, and a large amount of babying, is another psychological defense. In a culture that puts a premium on sickness, it is hard to keep even the pastor from seeking some of its rewards.

A third device is to succumb to self pity. No defense pays fewer dividends and none is less fitting for the pastor. When members of the parish refer to him as "poor Mr. Jones," he has already destroyed his spiritual usefulness. Pity is the emotion we feel toward the weak, and the pastor who exults in inner weakness is denying in his own life the values he should be proclaiming.

Another common escape is to become an ecclestiastical Levite, inundating life with trivial activities as substitutes for the real tasks of the ministry. Guilt over failure to face the large tasks with courage is placated by the self-punishment that comes through enslavement to the menial and trivial.

Until a man can face the deep meanings of his behavior, he is not living a mature and examined life. The care of his own soul of souls, his inner core of being, his citadel of spirit demands the courage and candor to look at himself honestly.

The four examples at the beginning of this chapter show unresolved problems with roots beyond the reach of self-examination and self-treatment. There are other problems, however, which men can learn to handle with wisdom, as the two examples that follow will illustrate.

Ellsworth H. had specialized in pastoral counseling. He enjoyed that part of the work and did it well. However, the needs of the parish demanded calling in the homes of his people. He tried to avoid this duty, inventing excuses and rationalizing his inability to make these visits. Finally faced with a crisis among his people, he went to see the professor with whom he had studied counseling. Here in safe surroundings he confided that he tried to make such pastoral calls, sometimes even getting his finger on the doorbell before turning away in defeat. With his counselor he examined his feelings and their roots; he began to realize that he had a fear of people, of what they might think of him. Perhaps, he said, they might not want to accept him in their homes. During his conversations now he recognized traumatic experiences in his life which had evidently caused these apprehensions. When he discovered that he had been generalizing on the basis of false fears he started a program of self-training. He planned a few calls that he knew would work out well. He found himself comfortable with persons he had worked with in other relationships. He thought out his calls in advance so that he would be able to proceed without floundering. Then he tried more difficult visits, with newcomers and strangers. When he found he was accepted and welcomed he gained more courage. Two years later he was making numerous calls without difficulty, and to his own surprise found that he was actually enjoying it and applying his counseling skills in new and interesting settings.

Eugene W. had carried on an effective ministry for years. His church grew until he needed a full-time assistant. However, when he began working with the well-qualified and fine-spirited colleague who was assigned to share the parish with him, he found himself growing critical, resentful and jealous. He regretted and tried to cover up these unpleasant feelings. But when requests came from members for his associate to perform such pastoral duties as baptisms, weddings and funerals, Eugene could not handle his hostile reactions. He was smart enough, however, to recognize that he was dealing with an emotional problem within himself. He applied for membership in a group counseling program and during a period of several months talked out his feelings. He learned much about himself. He became aware of the fact that he had sought status and security in the position the pastor holds with his people. Sharing that position threatened him. When he understood that he did not have to defend himself against threats that did not really exist he became more comfortable and was able to share parish tasks with better feeling. His insight did not come all at once, and he had to work at the task of maintaining a right relationship with his colleague, but when he understood the causes for the effects that bothered him, he was on the way toward growth and a finer ministry.

When the varied selves within a man bend their energies toward a common goal, the roles the pastor is obliged to play as preacher, counselor, administrator, educator, family man and human being take on a new and unifying meaning. Then the pastor can properly care for himself because he is not the unwilling instrument of his contending selves, but a being totally dedicated to something beyond himself.

The tasks of ordination, dedication, and consecration are unending, since they involve growth. The pastor who is vitally alive and firm in his faith in himself and his mission possesses a fundamental resource that is not concealed; it is communicated in all he says and does and thinks and feels.

His ministry becomes commandingly relevant. All there is of him is engaged in the important task of mediating God's healing and redeeming revelation in a world troubled and suffering for the want of it.

2

PASTORAL CARE OF THE ILL

*P*ERHAPS there is no place where the pastor's confusion is greater than in his role in ministering to those who are sick. The minister often does not know whether he should serve Hygeia or Aesculapius.

Hygeia, the Greek god of health, symbolized the innate

quality of wholeness that moved a being toward the real-ization of his nature as a health-endowed being. Aescula-pius, the Greek god of healing, was dedicated to restoring the sick person to wholeness through the medical arts of repairing damage and disordered functioning.

This confusion is indicated by the changed meaning of the rite of unction. Originally it was the religious ritual by which the power of the church was placed behind the move toward organic health. With time its purpose changed until it became the act by which the disordered and broken crea-ture was sacramentally returned to his creator by the church. So what had orginally been the property of Hygeia became, by the processes of time, the property of Aescula-pius.

This same confusion reveals itself in relation to the pas-tor's function in the modern hospital setting. Should he seek to represent the role of health of being, or should he make himself a minor aide to the disciples of Aesculapius? Too often the church has abdicated its role as the champion of healthful functioning and has placed itself at the disposal of the practitioners of the art of healing, the disciples of Aescu-lapius. So the church puts its resources behind the hospital, gives it support financially and psychologically, as if this were its major contribution to the ministry of health and wholeness. The contribution that the church could make to the role of Hygeia usually goes begging.

Our culture is oriented about illness as a desirable escape from life. We grant rewards for illness that are not granted for health. We give support and sympathy to the sick. We give financial rewards for ill health and an approved status for those whose physical functioning has broken down. Breakfast in bed, tender love and care, floral tributes and expressions of concern are showered on the sick and withheld from the healthy. It is quite natural that people under stress should find this treatment inviting.

Even our definitions of health are approached from the angle of illness, as if wholeness of being were an absence of symptoms, rather than a state of dynamic functioning. Even the more positive definitions of health do not escape this body-oriented view. Foote and Cottrell in their book, *Identity and Interpersonal Competence,* speak of health as "the progressive maximization—within organic limits—of the ability of the organism to exercise all of its physiological functions, and to achieve its maximum of sensory acuity, strength, energy, coordination, dexterity, endurance, recuperative power and immunity." While such definitions move beyond the negative preoccupation with disease, they do not escape a preoccupation with organic functioning.

The New Testament view of health is more positive. It implies that the essence of health is an inner spiritual state that manifests itself in proper organic functioning. Jesus was a disciple of Hygeia. He never gave mere sympathy. While he recognized the presence of illness and disease, he never gave it "status" by dwelling on its negative aspects. Rather he sought to free the individual from the cause of his disfunction by offering him something more profound and worthy, "the faith that makes for wholeness." Until we find again this emphasis in our ministry to the sick, we are going to be enmeshed in an unwilling slavery to the disciples of Aesculapius.

Here, however, we are getting some valuable assistance from a branch of medicine that has become aware of some of the basic causes of ill health. Psychosomatic medicine is more concerned with understanding causes of illness than in treating the symptoms of organic breakdown. So at this point we are finding within the field of medical study and research a new awareness of the place of Hygeia.

Working under a Ford Foundation grant and under the auspices of Johns Hopkins Medical School, Dr. Jerome Frank and a corps of assistants have been studying the faith factor in the healing process. For a long time it had been observed that there were elements at work that were not due to any specific medication. When placebos, inert substances with no medicinal value, were adminstered, the patient often showed the same improvement one would have expected from the indicated medication. What factors were at work?

Writing of the findings of the study in the February, 1959 issue of the "Journal of Psychiatry," Dr. Frank identified these factors as expectancy, suggestion, status, and personality structure.

It was observed that in many instances the patient reacted in response to his own expectancy. When injections of distilled water, instead of morphine, were given to patients suffering from post-surgical pain, the patient relaxed and went to sleep with a marked decrease in his discomfort. The New Testament reports "that it was done to them according as they expected." Modern medicine verifies this organic response to expectancy.

Similarly, suggestion works to aid the healing process.

Patients who received an injection of saline solution, accompanied by a strong suggestion that they would not be troubled with the common cold, responded better than did those who were given the best cold serum available. Also, the prestige of the physician or the institution seemed to have a measurable effect on the patient; in other words, his trust in the competence and integrity of the administering agent had a bearing on his response. And the personality of the patient was also a factor, for some of them resisted the specific medication, while others willingly cooperated with all efforts to aid them toward health.

Special techniques were employed to understand what was at work in the personalities of those who resisted the efforts to heal them. They proved to be resistive, doubting and rigid. They used the resources of their personalities to cling to their ailments. Others who were faith-filled, cooperative, open, and accepting were willing and able to accept suggestion and create expectancy. (The latter are commonly referred to as "good patients," while the former are referred to by Flanders Dunbar as "the patients that make the doctor sick.")

When patients who were allergic to penicillin were invited to submit to injections of a new non-allergenic type of penicillin—but were actually injected with distilled water—some showed their usual allergic response to the distilled water. Some highly suggestible patients even reversed the result normally expected from the medication because of the suggestion and expectancy that was created in them; a number of patients suffering from nausea were given an emetic with the suggestion that it would settle their stomachs in no time at all—and it did.

Similarly, patients applying for psychiatric treatment were told that they could not be scheduled for psychotherapy at once, but would instead be given a drug to calm their emotions and make it possible for them to function normally. Imposing capsules with an inert substance were administered. And the patients showed marked improvement.

Such medically supervised experiments point out that there are factors at work in the healing process beyond and above mere chemical reaction. The glandular system that controls body chemistry is most sensitive to emotional stimuli, and when suggestion and expectancy are at work to help create right feelings, the whole organism shows the beneficial results.

The factors medically identified as elements of a working faith are well within the range of traditional religious interest. They have their independent value, and an understanding of how they work can do much to modify the clergyman's approach to the patient. They give a new relevance to those ministrations that are an important part of the pastor's work in mediating God's healing, redeeming love.

The pastor who understands his role can be instrumental in throwing the weight of religious practice and traditional religious thinking on the side of health rather than illness. In his book, *Persuasion and Healing,* Jerome Frank shows how important the religious impulse may be in healing; religious persuasion may be a major stimulant to the faith that moves a person toward wholeness.

The pastor's role is not one of competition with medical resources, but rather a wise cooperation with them. The practice of Christian Science in denying the validity of medicine is based on a philosophical premise demonstrably not shared by traditional Christian thought; Jesus did not deny disease or the validity of current medical practice. Quite the contrary: he seemed to employ it in making salves of the chemically rich soil of Palestine to apply to the eyes and other affected parts of those to whom he ministered. So can the pastor cooperate in every way possible with medical science, and yet at the same time be aware of the important healing ministry that he may perform, that he is, in fact, commissioned to perform, along with preaching and teaching.

In understanding disease it is important to understand causative agents. The history of medicine has shown differing approaches to the cause of illness. Aristotle and Galen thought of illness as disturbances of the elements and humors. They treated the whole being rather than the parts. This practice carried down to medieval times, as shown by Chaucer's characterization of the physician:

> "He knew the cause of every malady
> Where it is hot, or cold, or moist, or dry;
> And where engendered, and of what humour.
> He was a very perfect practiser."

Modern medical practice has been subject to the subtle encroachments of materialism. Such materialistic attitudes toward medical practice make it difficult or impossible to properly assess man's spiritual nature and its contribution to his illness or health.

Modern science is preoccupied with mechanics and applied physics; and medicine, as a branch of modern science, has in the last century shared this general mood. It considers man as an aggregate of mechanical parts interacting with each other. The individual is treated as a machine with a need for fuel, lubrication, and adjustment to keep it properly functioning. When one function breaks down, an effort is made to identify the offending part and to restore it to proper operation. This may involve modifying the body chemistry through medicine, or taking more drastic action against the offending part through surgical intervention. This preoccupation with parts has led to specialization, where physicians develop more and more knowledge about the function of individual organs. Such an approach has naturally moved away from a concern for the total being. As T. S. Eliot put it, "Where is the knowledge we have lost in information?"

However, a truer understanding of man seems to be emerging from a new interest in medicine combined with an old emphasis on religion. Emphasis on preventative medicine, along with a new revelation of the nonmaterial nature of reality, has led research beyond a mechanical interest in the parts to a study of the total being reacting to the whole process of living. Experiments with hypnosis have proved the power of thought over bodily function. The use of drugs as agents to produce relaxation gives further credence to the premise that emotional factors need to be controlled to bring organic functioning nearer to the norm.

Modern medicine is engaged in a major conflict between the organicists and those more concerned with emotional and functional etiology. Yet the more research that is done, the more it seems apparent that the total being is involved in every diseased state. All specialization ultimately has to face the fact that there is no physical state that is not affected by emotion, and no emotional state that cannot have its effect on the physical. They are indeed so inseparably bound together that it is difficult to tell where one ends and the other begins; ultimately they always travel together. So the role which traditional religion abdicated in favor of the medical practitioner is now being thrust back upon the pastor by those who are increasingly aware of man's spiritual nature and its relationship to his health.

There is a striking similarity between the concepts of a Park Avenue psychiatrist and an early church father. Origen wrote, just a few decades after the last of the New Testament was written, "for many, being overcome by trouble and not knowing how to bear sickness bravely, are proved then to be sick in soul rather than in their bodies." Dr. Gotthard Booth, the contemporary psychiatrist, says, "The old idea of 'normal people with a sick body' and of 'psychopathic people with a healthy body' has to be abandoned. There are only healthy and sick personalities."

With the importance now given to states of mind and emotion as factors in the development and management of disease, the pastor cannot ignore the part he plays on the team of professional persons who work to maintain or restore wholeness. No longer need the pastor creep hesitantly about the hospital, barely tolerated in the sacred precincts of the true healer. Over the main door of the Presbyterian Medical Center in New York are the words, "All healing is of God."

And today a new relevance is found in words of Jesus that emphasize the importance of the inner being. New meaning is found in those practices of the church that are continually at work to help people deal with their own emotions. It is seen now that worship is a major therapeutic resource for health of mind and spirit. Confession, meditation, group participation, and praise are ingredients of a normal, balanced way of life.

There are four causative agents of what we call illness. One is the aging process, and we will devote a later chapter to the special pastoral ministry to the aged; here it is enough to point out that important psychological factors are at work in the aging process, and that the life with interests, direction, and purpose slows up the aging process, while the life that is aimless and depairing shows rapid breakdown.

A second factor is environment. Variables as different as climate and culture, nutrition and radiation, germs and worms may be elements of this external world that affect the life of the individual who lives in it. The emotions of the individual are clearly established as important factors in protecting himself against the damaging effect of environment. The integrated personality seems to present a united front against destructive elements in environment while the disorganized and disintegrating personality has reduced resistance against intrusion from without.

A third source of illness is commonly referred to as the accident. Current study interprets many accidents as unconsciously planned behavior, with a small percent of accident-prone persons accounting for a major portion of the accidents. Suppressed self-destructive impulses and unmanageable feelings seem to be an important cause of what, for want of a better term, we continue to call accidents.

Related to this, in less dramatic form, are the emotions that work internally to produce disordered function with its end result of organic distress.

In all areas of health it is clearly established that emotional factors are at work. These emotional factors are often associated with an inadequate concept of life and its meaning, and a breakdown in human relations. Much of medical practice among the disciples of Aesculapius is given to the treatment of symptoms; but deep concern for values, adequate purpose, and right relations is prior and more basic, and is clearly within the range of pastoral interest.

We have tried to establish that illness is not just a matter of physical symptoms, that the role of the pastor with the sick is a distinct and important relationship not to be overshadowed by those who treat symptoms, and that the pastor who is aware of his role can make an important contribution on the team of those who work for true health and wholeness.

Now we want to indicate how this can be done. In the first place, the pastor never loses sight of the fact that he is a disciple of Hygeia. While he recognizes and cooperates with the disciples of Aesculapius, he recognizes the prior claim of the wholeness of life, and works always with this focus in his mind. In the second place, he is aware of the important preventative force that religion makes available through worship, confession, counseling, and group life. In the third place he knows that there is no physical condition that does not have an emotional reflection, and no emotional state that does not have its physical counterpart. As a specialist in those deep emotions that affect life, he is always aware of the important function he performs in restoring life to health and the being to wholeness.

To fulfill these important pastoral functions, the wise minister permeates the whole parish ministry with a belief in the value of health of body, mind, and spirit. Instead of creating an institution that adds values to illness by accepting it and glorifying it, he places emphasis upon sustaining health as well as restoring it when it is temporarily fractured.

Here then the pastor sees his function not as a meek and lowly intruder in the sacred halls of Aesculapius, but rather as the custodian of a way of life that continually enriches the healthy while helping those temporarily enmeshed in the state of being we call illness. To this end he seeks to know all he can about health and what sustains it; at the same time he is understanding of illness and the forces that overcome it. When the pastor accepts this attitude toward illness and the ill, he enters upon an important and fruitful aspect of his ministry, with the promise of great usefulness.

3

PASTORAL CARE
OF THE BEREAVED

A TIME of special pastoral privilege and responsibility
comes when the acute deprivation of death disrupts
the emotional lives of those whom we serve. This distressing
experience, an inescapable part of all human existence,
must be dealt with sooner or later by everyone. According

to the Social Security actuaries, two million people will die this year. Most of them will leave family, relatives, and close friends who feel the loss. Perhaps thirty million people a year are bereaved. This means that on the average every person in the country comes face to face with death in personal terms once every six years.

The wise and perceptive pastor accepts this privileged relation, aware of its difficulty but facing the difficulty because he knows this is a time when what he represents can prove itself in the testing. The pastor's ministry at the time of acute emotional stress affirms a faith that underlies all living, no matter what the incidental factors of that existence may be. As the agent of the community and its institutions, it is he who helps the bereaved individual face both the reality of what has happened and what can next happen. Moreover, the pastor becomes the instrument for wise handling of the deep emotions that are inevitable at times of personal crisis, and, by accepting them, he allows for their healthful handling.

Only in recent years have we been aware of the deep and far-reaching effects of grief. We have always known that it was prevalent, and that everyone must suffer from it sooner or later. But medical studies of recent years have traced many serious ailments back to the deep emotions related to grief, showing that there are reactions affecting body, mind, and spirit. The wise pastor is aware of these things and is prepared to take the action best suited to the needs of the individuals involved.

The deep emotions related to grief precipitate fears, anxieties, feelings of guilt, states of depression, and other threats to the basic health of the individual. The wise management of the grief syndrome becomes a major factor in protecting the physical and emotional well being of the mourner.

It was Dr. Erich Lindemann, professor of psychiatry at Harvard, who first directed attention to the significant physical results of unwisely managed grief. While doing a study of ulcerative colitis, he discovered that more than eighty per cent of the patients had had an mismanaged grief experience during the six months preceding the onset of the disease. Such statistical findings cannot easily be overlooked.

Dr. E. Weaver Johnson, in a book on psychosomatic medicine, comments that unresolved grief appears to be one causative factor in the onset of diabetes. The excessive demand on the glandular system for extended periods of time causes the glands to break down in function under the stress.

Dr. Lawrence LeShan, working under a grant of the Ayer Foundation at Trafalgar Hospital in New York, has been studying "spontaneous regressions" in malignancies. After eleven years of such study, he affirmed in an article in a professional journal that he had not done a depth analysis on any terminal patient whose emotional profile did not show as its main unconscious characteristic an unutterable despair. The roots of this despair, he indicated, appeared to be in many instances a bereavement that disorganized life and its meaning. This despair affected glandular reaction and body chemistry and in so doing may have permitted the irregular cell growth to get out of control.

These illustrations of recent findings, drawn from among many that could be cited, show that unwisely managed grief may be an important factor in producing physical symptoms. But the effects of grief may show up in behavior as well.

Dr. Rollo May, in his study "Anxiety," examined the behavior of fourteen adolescents who were considered delinquent. Eleven of the fourteen had lost a parent, or one who took the place of a parent, during their early years. There appeared to be a correlation between the angry behavior directed against society and the feelings of injustice and deprivation growing from the death of one upon whom the child had been emotionally and socially dependent.

What is true of physical symptoms and behavior may also be true of spiritual values. The death of a loved one may so thoroughly disorganize life that all forward motion is lost. This may lead to the activities that represent partial suicide, or in some instances suicide itself. We are all familiar with those news items in the daily press that conclude a story about a suicide with the statement, "Relatives say that Mrs. Smith has been despondent since the loss of her husband six months ago."

When we grant the important impact of grief upon life, we see more clearly the role of the pastor in helping to resolve the crises it precipitates. If we keep clearly in mind that bereavement is apt to be the most severe deprivation experience a person will ever face, we can then be better prepared to deal with the emotions that it lets loose.

Students of this deep emotion are in agreement that four important considerations must be kept uppermost in working with the bereaved.

First, it is important to remember that all of the religious and social rituals surrounding death are designed to meet the emotional needs of the survivors and have no purpose at all for the deceased. Therefore, the whole point in considering them is to try to understand what is happening to the mourners, and how these activities can help to meet their emotional needs.

One danger here is that we try to intellectualize about the deep emotions that go with grief, especially about the emotions of other persons. Without realizing it, some pastors reject the feelings of their parishoners by trying to prescribe how they should feel and how they should express their feelings at such times. This usually is done at the intellectual level. The deep feelings of life have their own integrity, and while we can think about them constructively, it is unreasonable to assume that we can think away the feelings. Intellectualization, when applied to our emotions, can be one of the more subtle forms of repression, and may so interfere with the normal expression of feelings that it becomes a contributive factor to the delayed effects that plague body, mind, and spirit.

Grief is an honorable emotion growing from the high value placed upon life. It is a complex emotion through which ambivalent feelings are often vented. Because it *is* deep, complex and powerful, it is unreasonable to suppress it. Often the ritualized activities surrounding the event make it possible for these strong feelings to be expressed—worked through—wisely and well. But in doing so it is always important to realize that we are working with *feelings*, not just thoughts or ideas, at least in the early stages of grief work.

The customs and practices of the community appear to have evolved from emotional necessity, for they minister to the deeper levels of consciousness from which the strong emotional responses come. For instance, there is no grief experience that is completely free from guilt feelings. When an important emotional relationship is fractured by death, the finality of the event forces one to contemplate the unfinished business of life, and the things that he might do better given another chance. But with death there is no other chance. One cannot now take back the unkind word spoken in anger or the careless act that came with fatigue. How often we hear people say, "Oh, if only I had known." If such feelings are unresolved and turned inward, they may become the tormenting self-anger that produces depression. It is helpful to have some final way of absolving one's self of the feelings of guilt that exist. Among some Jewish people the practice of speaking only good of the deceased for a week furnishes a way of expressing guilt and compensating for it in healthy ways. The acts of care for the body of the deceased are also ways of meeting this emotional need. A casket is a container for treasures. The outworn physical body may not seem to be a thing to treasure, and yet a last opportunity to show respect and consideration for the long-time residence of a deeply loved spirit may be a sufficient means of working through guilt feelings. And the casket is the last gift the living can give to the dead. It is better to express sentiments creatively, even though it may involve some monetary expense, than to carry a soul-shattering anger against the self that may cost infinitely more to work through with a psychiatrist. But expression of feelings usually does not follow clearly determined logical patterns. So it is wise not to try to impose logic on the emotions of others, for the emotions have their own validity, and usually find their own healthful expression if not interfered with.

A second matter of great importance is to aid the bereaved individual to keep a clear focus on the reality of what has happened. Distortion of reality is the seedbed in which emotional illness germinates. The clergyman's role is to affirm the reality while giving emotional and spiritual help in meeting it.

In all painful experience there is a tendency to seek escape. For example, acute physical pain often makes a person faint; this is a blotting out of consciousness at the point where consciousness has become intolerable. What is true physically is also true emotionally. A person can faint from fear or intolerable emotional pain. Or he can use his mental equipment to deny the reality of what has caused emotional pain. In a purely chemical sense, this may involve taking sedation to block the neural areas that control the feeling of pain. Sometimes a physician supplies the escape by medication, and sometimes an individual provides his own through that most easily available of all temporary pain killers, alcohol. This type of escape may divert the feelings or suppress them for a few hours, but in no instance does it serve a therapeutic purpose. The feelings continue to exist and must be met at one level or another, sooner or later.

It is the pastor's role to help people face the *full* impact of the physical fact of death. The church has traditionally been the institution in society that has not been afraid to be honest emotionally about death. Its scriptures and its hymns help men accept reality, sustained and soothed by an unfaltering trust. It is unfortunate when the pastor fails to see that his role is helping people to face reality and to use their inner resources to come to terms with it.

There has been a trend in recent years to make light of death. Because most deaths occur in hospitals, in the presence of professionally trained persons, the average person has little opportunity to know what it is. Because of the unreal atmosphere surrounding it, and for lack of wiser emotions concerning it, men make light of death and try to deny its reality for themselves. The inability to face the full impact of nuclear catastrophe is an example of this unreality attached to death. People do not feel that this horrible thing can be real, at least not for them.

Sometimes pastors unwittingly cooperate with this trend by employing a type of service that intellectualizes the process of death and detours around the painful facts to which people must adjust at the deepest levels of their beings. They counsel a quick disposal of the remains, and an unemotional service emphasizing spiritual values. This may appear wise at the intellectual level, but it fails to meet basic emotional needs. And it tends to ignore the realities which must be faced in order for the grief to be worked through normally. Such intellectualized approaches to grief are psychological sedation.

The deep emotions must be considered first, and grief is a deep emotion. A physician may say to the assembled family the fateful words, "John has expired." The ears may hear the words but the meaning may be muffled by feelings that refuse to accept the fact. While the conscious mind may understand the words, the deeper levels of consciousness, the levels where the feelings lie, may resist the painful meaning. The process by which the deep meaning is made real to the total being is of utmost importance at this time, for unless the feelings can be brought to the state of healthful expression, nothing that can be said to the rational being will assuage the grief.

It is for this reason that Dr. Lindemann emphasizes the therapeutic importance of "viewing the remains," for by this process the deeper levels of emotion are reached in a way that verbalization alone cannot produce. While some of the practices that are emotionally distressing could well be eliminated from funeral practice, it would not be wise to eliminate those that serve the necessities of the deep feelings. While public viewing after the religious service is inappropriate, the experience of affirming the reality of the physical fact by those most closely involved emotionally is a valuable aid in the therapeutic process.

It has been observed repeatedly that the type of funeral service that denies the next of kin the chance to do this simple act prolongs the grief and often creates delayed reactions that are more difficult to cope with. The reaction of families during wartime, when memorial services were the only possibility, have indicated that the emotions of the bereaved organize themselves about illusions and false judgments, and until these emotional states are resolved it is impossible to get on with the important tasks of living. It would be unreasonable to do from choice what necessity has shown to be unsatisfactory.

Akin to the matter of facing reality is the need for accepting the feelings that exist at such times. Often we are led to believe that repressed feelings are a sign of bravery, and sometimes we misguidedly urge people to control their feelings and hold back their tears. Emotions have their own status in life. The question is not whether they will or should be expressed, but simply whether they will be expressed wisely and well.

The feelings that come with grief may vary from excessive dependence to extreme anger and hostility. Often they involve guilt and show themselves in states of anxiety and depression. Such feelings are usually of short duration and work themselves out if given a fair chance. But to repress such strong feelings would prolong emotional problems. Those who work with mourners should help to make it possible for the bereaved to work through their feelings as rapidly as possible.

It is clear to the student of grief that this deep emotion grows from a fractured relationship. The pastoral role helps to support the person with fractured emotions until the healing powers within are able to set the person free of the past and prepare him for the future. This opportunity for quiet witness and continuous affirmation of the meaning of life reveals something not terminated by death; it is a generator of the values that are not touched by anything incident to the existence that is measured by space and time. The fractured relationships of time are healed in the values of the timeless, and the promise of a more abundant life in the spirit is not something for the future but is, rather, the achievement of the mourner who faces his grief and finds in it the power to become even now a Son of God, a joint heir with Christ.

An important first step in this direction is for the spiritual counselor to accept the feelings that are expressed, and to make it clear that he values the feelings for what they are, a deep anguish of the soul. When he accepts these feelings, it becomes easier for the mourner to accept and express his own feelings. When this is done, a major step is taken toward resolving them.

The traditional funeral service provides the setting within which feelings can be easily expressed. In every culture, from the most primitive to the most advanced, one of the major characteristics of the human being is that he buries his dead with ceremony. All of the important events of life are surrounded by rites and rituals that make it possible for individual and group emotions to be expressed. A wedding is just as legal when performed by a justice of the peace, but most people choose to give this event in life the most sacred and significant setting possible. A baptism implies the sacredness of young life. A funeral similarly symbolizes the sacredness with which life is viewed. It gives the community an opportunity to express its feelings and to accept the feelings of those who are going through a personal crisis.

So the fourth important thing to remember in ministering to the grief-stricken is the need for an appropriate set of events and ceremonies as the channel through which the community expresses its feelings, and, in so doing, gives support to the valid emotions of the bereaved.

Often we wonder about the things people say at such times, statements sometimes tinged with superstition and inanity. But through it all comes a strong feeling that words cannot express, that there is a common bond among the living as they face the mystery of death.

The pastor who has a deep perception of the movement of emotion in the lives of his people can be of great aid to them in meeting the crises of life. Indeed, at no point can he be more useful than in ministering to those who face the mystery of life and death. These mourners stand at a point of spiritual vulnerability. Dr. Herman Feifel has pointed out that among persons over fifty years of age the main preoccupation of the subconscious mind, as revealed through projective testing, is the subject of one's own death. When the bell tolls, very truly, "it tolls for thee."

To be able to administer the rites and rituals that provide a healthy outlet for deep feelings, to affirm the realities as a foundation for building a revised life, to value and encourage the expression of deep feelings, and to bring to the suffering individual the wise and sustaining support of the community—these important aspects of grief therapy are entrusted to the pastor.

A closing word on this subject about an opportunity that is sometimes missed: Dr. Lindemann says that the critical time in the mourning process comes about ten days or two weeks after the death. By that time friends and relatives usually have gone back to their regular activities. But the minister who is aware of the special needs can at this time be available to assume his pastoral responsibilities, to mediate God's healing, to offer redeeming love when it is most needed.

4

PASTORAL CARE
OF THE SHUT-IN

NEARLY EVERY PARISH has its list of shut-ins, usually people suffering from some form of physical ailment that keeps them at home. Most often they are the aged and infirm, and in some instances they include some suffering from senile dementia. With such people a pastoral call may be fruitful or meaningless, depending upon circumstance. Some do not recognize the pastor, or, if they do, forget that he has been there the moment he leaves. For others, though, this contact with the outside world is a breath of life. It makes them aware that they have not been forgotten, that they still have a life that is not separated from the things they once knew and shared with others.

Perhaps our whole idea of the shut-in needs to be re-examined in the light of our understanding of people and their behavior, for many shut-ins could more aptly be called "shut-outs." Do we ever take time to examine the process by which a shut-in becomes a shut-in, or similarly how a shut-out becomes a shut-out?

Since only half the people in this country have any church relationship, and since only a third of these are actively engaged in the church's life, we must be aware that the majority have voluntarily or involuntarily separated themselves from the major activities of the church. They are the shut-outs.

The importance of a relationship to the forces that can strengthen life and give it meaning is emphasized in the New Testament. Jesus was concerned with reaching the separated. The introductory chapter on the theology of relationship indicated this New Testament concern; we repeat that it must be a living interest in the pastoral ministry today. Ours is not merely to sit and wait for those who come to us with their problems, as important as that part of the ministry may be.

Ours is also to seek out those who are separated from the source that gives meaning to life.

Let us look briefly at some of the ways by which persons become separated from the sources of life's meaning.

Wendel K. was badly scarred about the face and chin in an airplane accident. His physician suggested that he allow his beard to grow to cover the ugly scars. The beard came out full and red. It actually made him look distinguished, and he attracted considerable attention in the neighborhood because of his unusual appearance. When people took a second look at him, Wendel assumed that they were passing judgment upon him. Basically quite a sensitive person, he became more so as his unusual appearance set him apart. His emotional response carried this separation a step further, and he withdrew more and more from the company of others. Although a young man in his early twenties, he avoided other young people. He lived alone and spent his evenings reading or watching television. He would be far from the usual classification of shut-in, but circumstances of life separated him from the human relations that sustain and develop the social being.

The circumstances that affected Fred L. were quite different. Too young to operate a car with a senior license, he illegally used his junior license after dark, and had an accident. In panic, Fred left the scene. He was subsequently caught, tried, and sent to a reform school. At the end of the required time he was released from the reformatory, but the inner release mechanism did not work. He could not escape the feeling that everyone knew him to be an ex-convict. His guilt and discomfort so overwhelmed him that he could not find the inner resources to relate himself again to society. Nor did neighbors make it easier; they warned their own youngsters against associating with him, lest they pick up habits and attitudes attributed to reform school living. Fred found it hard to talk with anyone; more and more he withdrew into a shell of self-imposed seclusion. In the midst of a culture with adequate resources to help him grow into new life, he became a psychic hermit.

Ellen was an attractive girl of sixteen. She was caught in an indiscreet act in the parking lot behind the railroad station. Within a short time, nearly everyone in her school knew about it. The boy involved was expelled from school and Ellen was compelled to have psychiatric examination and treatment. Almost immediately the girls of the school shunned Ellen because they were afraid they might be tainted by the association with her. The boys, in contrast, showed Ellen more attention than ever, though it was a type of attention that was disconcerting to Ellen and misinterpreted by the other girls. Ellen was made to feel completely excluded from any supportive associations at the time she most needed to be strengthened by such human relations. She was confused, frightened by what had so quickly happened to change the entire pattern of her life, and uncertain about how to redirect her life. She felt guilty, judged, and abandoned. She was aware that the attitude of her schoolmates had become prevalent in the youth group of the church. So she withdrew more and more from any group life, and finally left school to seek employment in a near-by city. In the midst of great need she was rejected, excluded, and uprooted from the very forces that could have helped to stabilize her life and move her into the future with self-respect and increased maturity.

Mrs. Ellis W. was sixty-six and in good health. She had always been active in church affairs. Her husband died, and for a few months she continued to be busy; but the difficulty of travel interfered with her activities. Always before her husband had provided her transportation. After his death, neighbors arranged to help her out, but she was sensitive about asking for rides, and by a slow process lost touch with things. Her problem was not acute and she suffered no severe pangs of social separation. She just gradually shared less and less and cared less and less. Once in a while someone would call on the phone or stop by, but Mrs. W. was not the talkative type, and before long this interest in her withered away. By the end of a year she was almost completely shut off from the interests and activities that had been such an important part of her living. She was shut-in —not because of any physical condition, but because of a social accident. She had just drifted away when no one was looking, and once the contacts were broken, it was too much effort to try to establish them again.

A study made of persons outside the organized group life of the community shows that the main reasons for separation are not dissimilar to those Jesus referred to in the three stories of the separated ones; the accidental loss illustrated by the coin, the careless loss depicted by the sheep that wandered away, and the deliberate separation shown by the wilful son. In each instance, the separation caused a breakdown in function and usefulness, and it was necessary for restoration to take place before life could be productive again. With the accidental and careless separation, it took group effort to help restore the separated. Where the separation was deliberate, there had to be an initial act by the wilful son, but there also had to be a waiting community ready and willing to restore the son to his rightful place in the midst of a sustaining family.

People separated from the life of the church, those shut-in by circumstance or shut-out by choice, represent a major claim upon the pastor's interest.

Sometimes these separated persons cry for help, and there is none. Or they seek it in strange places and have to be helped back to the more normal way of life.

Mrs. Van was in her middle eighties, a widow on county aid. She had one room in a private home, with the privilege of using the kitchen when the household had gone to work. The pastor was called in to consider the problem of the old lady who was doing such strange and careless things as leaving doors open in winter and the stove lighted under empty kettles. She seemed incoherent, but also as pleasant and gracious a little old lady as one could imagine, quite the prototype of Whistler's mother. A doctor was called to give a more detailed examination, and she was taken to the county home for psychiatric examination, presumably for senile dementia.

In about a week the psychiatrist called the pastor and said, "You can come and get your old lady. We are discharging her." The pastor asked for details and was bluntly told that "as soon as the alcohol had been gotten out of her system, the old lady was quite all right again." In talking with Mrs. Van the pastor found that she had not had a drink in her life until about a year before the events described. She said she felt so lonely she didn't know what to do, and she had heard that a drink would make one feel better. She tried it and had been drinking steadily and increasingly for months. She kept her secret by hiding her empty bottles in neighbors' garbage cans. When place was found for her in a home for folks of her own age, she gained a new interest and a new life. The symptom of her loneliness has not re-occurred. A separated one was restored to human fellowship.

Quite in contrast was Mrs. Rose, a young woman in her early thirties. She had married a man of Roman Catholic faith who did not believe in family planning. In eight years of married life Mrs. Rose had six children. The family income was limited and the never-ending tasks of a family of eight on a limited budget waged a war of attrition upon the soul of Mrs. Rose. Mrs. Rose had no place to go and nothing to wear if she did. She could not afford a baby sitter and her husband preferred to stay home evenings anyway. The year-in, year-out drudgery made Mrs. Rose feel sorry for herself. She knew few people in the community, and really didn't care to know anyone. She was becoming separated and depressed when she heard a local pastor speak over the radio. In his talk he mentioned that there is a solution to nearly every problem, if we can work wisely toward finding it.

Mrs. Rose called the pastor and asked him to visit her. In brief, she asked, "What do you do with a problem like mine? I resent my husband and his inconsiderate attitude. I love my children but need a break once in a while. I get so tired I think I can't get through another day, but I have to because there is no one else to do what has to be done. So, where is the solution to this problem?"

Mrs. Rose talked out her feelings to the pastor, and through this alone began to feel less separated from an institution she had known in the past. Members of a young mothers' group in the church visited Mrs. Rose and talked with her about common interests, and again she felt related and supported in her feelings. She was asked to join the group. She gained the courage to talk over her needs with her husband and he agreed to baby-sit on the evenings she attended group meetings. In a few months Mrs. Rose joined the church and took a new interest in herself and her life. Her despair and loneliness was bridged by a chance word over the radio and the series of events that led to active group participation. Those who are separated can be restored, and the cry for help is an important sound to hear.

We make a mistake if we think of shut-ins as the aged and infirm. Many of those who suffer most from loneliness and separation are young. Mrs. Rose was as much in need of someone to help her as was Mrs. Van. The young man with the scarred face, the young lad trying to find his way back to normal life after a period in a reformatory, the young girl who was excluded because of indiscretion, and the elderly widow who let life drift away from her because she hesitated to ask for transportation are examples of people who are cut off from life by circumstances that are often not easily controlled.

Physical illness is often a failure of relationship. Sometimes the condition of the shut-in is clearly a behavior manifestation—a person asking for neurotic rewards that he does not feel can be obtained in any other way. A wheel chair does not appeal to most of us, but for some, because it gains attention, it is a reward.

It would be an interesting exercise for the pastor to take a dozen names from his list of shut-ins and examine the needs and interest of these people, not from the usual superficial approach taken in most parishes, but rather with a depth of perception that seeks to understand the person, his personality, how he became the way he is and what could be done to help him find new and interesting life.

Then it might be wise to go over the membership of the parish and set down in a special list those who have drifted away from group life. A carefully planned effort could be made by a trained visitation committee to meet with these people, casually, to find out what is going on in their lives. In this way it might be possible to find out where the church has failed them. The assumption we sometimes make that everyone should attend church regularly—and is a spiritual delinquent if he does not do so—needs to be examined. There is just as much warrant for believing that the church fails its people as that the people fail the church. If the church is a means toward an end, it must continually examine itself to test whether it is truly seeing real people as they live. Or is it carrying on a meaningless program to which some people, for inadequate reasons, continue to give half-hearted support?

The ministry to the separated can be one of the richest facets of the church's life. The membership of the parish can be trained to be alive to the needs of those who are having trouble relating themselves to life. Special interests can be developed for youth, the student population, the transients, and the middle-aged, as well as for the aged. It hurts to be lonely at any age. The life of the parish can be organized to make people feel valued and important, so that they grow in relationships as they participate in them.

The person who is shut-in by circumstance is more clearly defined than the selective shut-in, but the *needs* are no more clearly defined. Both need to relate to something beyond the self. The psychic hermit is passing a judgment on society, and for him the judgment is an outgrowth of experience. Whether his experience is normal or not is not the question for us; it is real to him, and for him the reality of it is paramount. The more acute the separation, the more perceptive must be the observer, and the more skilled in helping in the process of restoration.

Almost as if to justify a lack of concern, some people raise the question, "But what if a person wants to be separated? Doesn't he have a right to turn his back on others if he wants?"

Wait; there is a prior and more important consideration. How can a social being live apart from the society that gives his life meaning? Society, for instance, intervenes to protect a person from himself when his depressed feelings show the threat of suicide. The less dramatic acts that involve partial suicide are no less significant merely because they do not pose as immediate a threat to life. Jesus went to those who were suffering exclusion and helped them back to right relations with some group. It might be the mentally ill, the physically ill or the socially ill. But in each instance Jesus was willing to take the initiative if necessary.

The church stands in society to minister to the needs of

men at the point where their social life seeks a cosmic dimension. It does not merely stand and wait. It believes so clearly in the inter-relationship between man's social and spiritual nature that it seeks just as vigorously to reach out to those who have needs and do not know it as to those who have needs and do know it.

Often the person who separates himself from the life of a sustaining group is admitting defeat. He feels he has failed as a human being. He may not express his feeling in such precise concepts, but within himself he suffers from the atrophy of an important part of his nature. The church is alive in society to help find those who suffer from such a withering away of spirit, and set them again in the midst of those who can nourish and sustain the social and spiritual being.

The shut-in or the shut-out may be suffering from grief, loneliness, or an uncontrolled resentment against some aspect of social life. He may feel guilt and be suspicious of those who, he feels, are judging him mercilessly. He may be suffering from a physical, a social or a psychological accident. He may have been so injured by society that he is protecting his wounds. But in his separation, whatever may be its cause, the sensitive ear can hear a call for help. Then is no time to pass by in unconcern, but rather a time to bind wounds and restore to life.

5

PASTORAL CARE OF CHILDREN

IN NO OTHER AREA has the insight of recent years done more to fortify the insights of the New Testament than in the understanding of children. The attitude that Jesus showed toward children appears all the more radical when we realize that it was more advanced than the

83

perception of many of our modern psychologists. To think that this understanding of the importance of childhood years emerged from a culture where children had no status and were considered only as potential assets until they reached their productive years is all the more remarkable.

Unfortunately, the history of the Christian church shows little awareness of the insight of the New Testament, and only in the past century has the church shown concern for Christian education of children. Understanding the importance of early years in the development of personality has stimulated a re-examination of both concepts and methods of guidance and nurture of children.

Four innovators in recent decades have thrown light on the processes by which the personality of the child is formed. Because their findings are relevant to our pastoral concern for children we will consider them briefly as a preface to this chapter.

Sigmund Freud first made us aware of the importance of the preconscious, subconscious and unconscious mind as a determinant of behavior. In connection with this exploration of the unconscious came the knowledge that practically all the experiences of the first three or four years of life are stored in the unconscious alone. Very little of this early experience can be recalled. But all that happened in these years has its impact on the personality.

In his exploration of disturbed states, Freud found that many emotions were rooted in early childhood experience. Perhaps there is no better illustration of this than Freud's own experience with religion. Born of a strict Jewish family in the rigid cultural pattern of Vienna, he had a strong set of feelings about the Jewish community and its religious faith and practice. But his nurse was a devout Roman Catholic who indoctrinated her young charge with the ideas and practices of her faith. This set up a deep inner conflict that Freud was never completely able to resolve. His social concern and the mystical quality of his nature indicated a strong religious leaning. Yet he fought against this quality in an attempt to resolve the inner emotional conflict growing out of his early impressions.

In spite of Freud's avowed atheism, he had a deep concern for religion, and the preoccupation in his writings with this subject shows how his inner conflict was seeking to resolve itself. In his book, *The Future of an Illusion,* he tries to explain away the force of religion in life, yet the illustrative material is steeped in what appear to be childish misconceptions of both the Jewish and Christian traditions. His last book, *Moses and Monotheism,* is an effort to relate the insights of his psychoanalytic discoveries with the Jewish tradition, but in this last effort his assaults are even less assured and his conclusions even more tentative. Had he been given more time, and had he lived in an era when the prevailing scientific mood was other than materialistic and mechanistic, his findings might well have been different.

The significance of his ideas were the impetus for more detailed studies by others of the growth and development of emotions and their effects upon behavior. At the very least they have compelled all of us to pay more attention to what is said and done to children in the pre-verbal years. For what a child cannot verbalize, he cannot usually recall; yet all this experience, often charged with strong emotion, is stored away at the deep levels of personality *and may influence behavior for years to come.* Such early experiences as the deprivation that comes with weaning, the insecurity that comes with separation from parents, the threat to love that comes with younger brothers and sisters, all produce strong emotional responses. Rarely can a person explain how his feelings developed; nevertheless there is no way of denying their importance and our need for careful examination of them.

Two of Freud's students have given special thought to the childhood influence on the adult personality. His daughter, Anna, became a specialist in the field of child psychiatry, and tried to develop the more orthodox interpretation of her father's ideas. Otto Rank, on the other hand, broke sharply with his teacher about the nature and influence of both religion and early childhood experience. In his book, *The Physician and the Soul,* Rank states that sex itself is not sufficient motivation for understanding what happens in the developmental process of life. In *Birth Trauma* he tries to trace back influences on the personality to the actual event of birth itself.

Rank's thesis is that birth itself is the critical emotional experience of existence. Before birth the the child lives in a safe, secure, perfectly contained and blissful world, where every need is satisfied and where there is no hazard except the growth process itself. Growth makes the little world too small to contain the growing life. In the act of emerging from the cozy and comfortable womb into the cold and threatening world, the baby endures an experience that is exceedingly painful and can actually be fatal. The first act of life is often a bellow of anger and rage. Being deprived of all that has sustained life in the past is a threatening event. In the thinking of Rank, the trauma associated with this experience is a major factor in the basic development of a personality. His study correlated the serene emotional nature of children born of easy births or of Caesarian sections with the emotionally disturbed patterns shown by those who had had unusually painful births. While his findings may be more specifically relevant for the therapist than for the pastor, it is important to understand that even this remote experience in life can be a factor in determining the way the person develops, and therefore significant in explaining adult behavior.

Nandor Fodor, the Hungarian psychoanalyst, has carried this idea one step further back. In his two major works, *The Search for the Beloved* and *The New Interpretation of Dreams,* he develops the idea that the psychic sensitivity that exists between mother and unborn child may be a significant factor in determining the emotional development of the personality. On the basis of studies of telepathy and the direct communication of emotion from subconscious mind to subconscious mind, he postulates that no relationship is closer than that which binds mother and unborn child. So the attitude of the mother toward the unborn child may determine how the child feels about himself later in life.

In his book on dream interpretation, he points out that the dream is the mirror of the unconscious and speaks its own symbolic language. In the analytic process he found again and again material that did not seem to be related to the life experience of the individual. But by correlating this material with the attitude of the parent toward the unborn child, he thought he found a clue to its reasonable explanation. For instance, a child who was unwanted, and toward whom the mother had harbored persistent resentment and even hatred (sometimes showing itself in unsuccessful attempts at abortion), carried through life a reservoir of low self-esteem and self-destructive hatred. On the other hand, the child who was planned for and eagerly and lovingly awaited, appeared to have a backlog of self-acceptance and assurance upon which the growth of the personality along healthy lines could be expected. Whether this theory is sound is not for us to determine here, but surely if we consider the possibility of subconscious communication between mother and child, it can broaden our thought concerning the important period of gestation.

Jean Piaget, in a series of significant books, has examined the emergence of personality, consciousness, conscience, and language in the young child. After careful observation of large numbers of children, he has concluded that the significant patterns of personality that persist through life are well established before the child is five years old.

Such insights coming from the careful studies of child development have important implications for the pastor. He is forced to realize that the traditional programs for child education in the church are apt to come along with too little, too late. This is borne out by a study of the results of parochial school education on the personalities of Roman Catholic children. Two years after graduation, apart from certain content material that had been learned, no discernible difference was found in the basic presuppositions about life between parochial school students and Catholics who attended public schools. This tends to confirm the idea that the basic presuppositions about life are not the product of formal education, but of those important earlier relationships that strongly effect the emotional quality of life itself.

This, then, directs attention toward the pastor's role in relation to the children of his parish. While he can be an important aid in directing life and resolving many of its problems among the children, his major effective role will be in parent education. This may start with premarital education, with the understanding that young adults have about their role as parents.

Much of the damage done to the emerging personality is done through ignorance and lack of understanding of the significance of the early years. Much of the so-called teaching of religion is merely a projection of adult hazards into the lives of young children. This can be illustrated by an examination of the impact of such early religious instruction; the illustrations may seem extreme, but counseling experience indicates that it is more common than we dare to imagine.

A man in his fifties came for counseling for an emotional problem. He was engaged in one of the most manly of occupations, but was overcome by a deep anxiety that showed itself in an acute fear of going to bed. Night after night he would pace up and down beside his bed for an hour or more before he could force himself to lie down, and then in terror and cold sweat he would suffer for hours through the night. He said that he could not go on in this way, that he felt he was on the verge of a nervous breakdown and had to have help.

In the counseling process he explored his feelings and their relationship to his behavior. Space makes it possible to record only some of the relevant conclusions. His mother had died just before the onset of the symptoms. His earliest recollection of his mother was of kneeling beside her to say a prayer about "dying before he awoke." Through the fifty years of his life he had always used this childhood prayer with the addition of the Lord's Prayer each evening. By this process he was able to feel close to his mother, and with the years this act had become symbolic, with the bed in effect symbolizing his mother's knee. With her death, his grief, his fear, and his anxiety produced an emotional crisis. The religious instruction that had given a false idea of prayer, and had planted deep within his mind an equation of bed equals dying, made him afraid to go to bed for fear his own death would ensue. When he was able to work through his feeling, and examine its meaning, his inner controls were strengthened and his free-floating fear was anchored at a point where he could do something about it. The efforts to relate highly subjective ideas to the concrete images of childhood can produce rotten fruit for a long time to come.

The ways by which children learn of religion are largely indirect and often subtle. Unpleasant rest rooms and an unkempt appearance about the church school building can be as significant, perhaps more so, than the words droned by an uninspired and uninspiring church school teacher. The attitude of parents toward the church school can have more influence on the child than anything the school staff can do. The child continually makes comparisons between church school and public school, between the attitudes of parents and teachers, between the atmosphere of church and other community buildings. While the results of his contrasts and comparisons may not be made articulate, they are nevertheless registered at the place where his feelings are recorded. These feelings come into play automatically when circumstances trigger them. The educational process goes on all of the time, and the formal program of the church is set in the midst of more powerful forces that are continually at work.

Jesus maintained a free and open approach to the children he met. This affronted his disciples, who felt that adults deserved the attention. Too often we are like those disciples, concerned about the adult's attitudes toward property, money, and program resources. We often act as if we thought chairs were more important than children. But chairs can be replaced; children alone are the raw material out of which God's kingdom can be built. They are indispensable and irreplaceable.

In view of the importance of childhood experience and the general practice of the church, what should be the pastor's role as he considers the children and how they grow? A re-evaluation of the pastor's time in relation to the children and youth of the parish is necessary. How many pastors welcome the opportunity to sit down and talk with young children? In how many parishes is it taken for granted that such procedure is unwelcomed, if not forbidden, because the pastor is "too busy"? How sad, for it is an interesting experience to sit down with really young children to share their enthusiasms, try to understand their questions, and offer answers that may have interest for the growing edge of their lives.

At what point within the parish program can truly sound attitudes toward children be developed? What can the pastor do to help parents understand the importance of being absolutely honest with children when they ask the first questions about the meaning of life itself? What does the church do to religious development of the child when it participates in those deceits worked upon children at Christmas time and Easter?

Such questions are a starting point for re-evaluating the total program of the church in its relation to its children. Honestly to face our shortcomings will help us move beyond the long-tried and proven failures that have resulted in innoculating children against real religion.

A program with children can best be started long before they are born—in other words, through work with prospective parents. The development of a well-rounded personality with a religious dimension is not something that can grow from a token act of confused and inadequate instruction. Rather it must be developed through a humble and appreciative approach to those sacred areas of life that come with the early years.

The primary aim of such a program should be to help parents learn how to communicate love to the child in an understandable, acceptable way—communicating it so plainly that the child learns early to accept and value himself, to respect his own identity. Long before the idea-creating and accepting equipment is working, feelings are shaping life, and these feelings are the important starting point for any program with children. Too much effort has been made to develop programs into which children are fitted. Instead we should first find out what is happening within the children and then build the program. Often, all that is needed is to be quiet enough to hear the child's questions. Such questions are the growing edge of the child's life. Responsiveness to his growing needs gives relevance to any program. Ignoring these needs makes any program irrelevant.

CHILD-CENTERED

Any program that waits for the child to be verbally competent, however, wastes the best years of life. This means that it is particularly important to emphasize parent education so that the privileged moments that come in the early years of life are not lost or ignored. Just as religion is primarily a matter of the deep feelings for life, so the religious development of the child begins with the first feelings he has about himself, his world, and the people who share it with him. The pastor who is aware of his role in enhancing the sacredness of young life and the rich feelings of its earliest years can make a major contribution to the lives of those who are children or are having children.

The baptismal admonition to teach by precept and example is a charge not only to parents but also to the church, which tries to make the sacrament of baptism an important recognition of a divine partnership in parenthood and in Christian nurture as well.

Christian education is not so much program as people. Children are people before they are born, and they become increasingly responsive through the years if those first fine moments of realization are filled with wise acceptance and true love. But this must always be love as the child understands it and not as the adult would phrase it, for in the years of early life communication is direct and powerful. The richly shared times of love and warm acceptance become the foundation upon which a life of growth, maturity, and realization can be built. Here is the foundation for education for life, and this should be the essence of any program of Christian education.

6

PASTORAL CARE OF YOUTH

*T*HE YOUNG PERSON in the parish has special
needs. The time of turbulent emotions comes with
a rush. And although much is expected of our young people,
often too little is done to help them meet the critical needs
of this period of their lives.

In his youth a person is expected to make the three most significant choices of his life, but he must do so with limited experience and in the midst of circumstances that are often confusing. It is difficult enough to go through a period of rapid change and multiple choices under the best circumstances, but in our day the external conditions add little to a state of serenity and objective calm.

Many of our young people have never known a time in their lives when the world about them was not seething in social and political crises. World conditions, with the prospects of destruction, raise doubts as to the security of the future, and sometimes make careful planning of a personal type seem irrelevant. Like the moth with a three-hour life span emerging from its cocoon in the midst of a hurricane, they see that life on this planet is far from secure and comfortable.

A youth is expected to choose a life work, a marriage partner, and a philosophy of life during these years. Yet the atmosphere for calm and objective discussion of his feelings with his parents is often less than ideal. Many parents are apprehensive about the future of young people, and feel that their own in particular are less ready and likely to accept advice and counsel than others. Under such conditions an open and frank approach to the pastor may be most helpful.

The problem of selecting life work is compounded by a baffling maze of choices. At one time it was enough to stay on the farm, or learn one of the professions, or become apprenticed at a trade. Now the pressure is to become an engineer or technician in any one of a number of scientific specialties. In the field of electronics there are hundreds of specializations, and in chemical engineering alone the special fields of study number nearly two thousand. Many young men are under pressure from industrial scouts who recruit promising students for their line of work. The competition for scholarships granted by industry makes it seem that this is the field that warrants most attention. But the endowment of the individual, his personal goals for living, and the type of employment that would lead to long-time satisfaction need to be considered. To be able to sit down with his pastor to talk casually about his interests can help to clarify goals as well as to raise questions that might otherwise not be considered. One pastor makes an appointment with each high school senior in his parish at the beginning of the last year in school, to see if he can be of help in making some choices. He does not neglect to mention the possibilities in religious work where it seems desirable. He assumes it is just as important to recruit worthy candidates for the ministry as it is to allow them to be recruited by industry.

Also, the important decision of a marriage partner is well within the pastor's interest. Through planned sessions with youth groups, matters relating to sex, courtship, and marriage can be raised. In a culture that commercializes sex, it is easy for young people to have an inadequate perspective on the role of sex in the total relationship that leads to marriage. Many young people who want to give the impression of being sophisticated are actually uncertain and perplexed about their relations with the opposite sex. They hear talk at school; they hear lectures at home that may be filled with threats; they see moving pictures and watch television

romance—and from it all there emerges little that is sound
and satisfying. The pastor has the privilege of pre-maritial
counseling. Yet as valuable as this may be, there is a need
for thought even before the final choice is made, for by then
it may be too late to resolve some of the problems that develop with interfaith marriages and incompatible back-
grounds. In helping young people approach this important
decision, it should be pointed out early in the game that a
sound marriage must have these three essentials: effective
communication, large areas of compatability, and soundness
of character.

Young people hear of new philosophies of life and they
wonder about them. If they have no basis for comparison,
they may not understand what existentialism really is. They
may get the idea that their impulses are the law of life, and
without proper guidance may damage their futures before
they have a chance to live them. Many young people do
not realize that only a small segment of the existential movement is atheistic and nihilist. They may be relieved to know
that Martin Buber represents an important mood of Jewish
thought, and Jacques Maritain develops existential thought
within the bounds of Roman Catholic tradition, and that
Kirkegaard and Tillich do the same for the Protestant tradition. In their need to understand current philosophical
thought, the pastor may be the only one who will interpret
the alternatives for them. A series of sessions with young
people on the main emphases of modern philosophy in relation to religion can help them clarify their thinking and
preserve their intellectual integrity in the midst of conflicting claims and counterclaims.

The pastor may be the chief defender of the young person's quest for meaning in life in the parish. Too often the youth of the church think they are considered as second class citizens, frowned upon because they want too much and give too little. In their minds, the attitude shown toward them becomes the indication of their worth. If the church fathers decide that chairs are more important than young people, the young people will find some place that puts a higher value upon them. If they are compelled to fit into a prescribed program that makes little place for their own thinking and acting, they will go elsewhere. If the judgment of their parents is taken as final in all matters, they will lose sight of the fact that they, too, are people.

Young people are constantly testing the boundaries of their living. It is important to understand what goes on in their minds and emotions. Anna Freud and Peter Blos have provided careful studies of the adolescent personality, which can be explored with profit. If it is understood that the sometimes erratic behavior of youth is one of the manifestations of normal neurosis, it will be easier to interpret it. Due to major glandular changes, the body chemistry is not always perfectly balanced, and this reflects itself in unbalanced behavior. The same thing is true of involution, change of life, and senescence. It becomes quite a problem when one household is afflicted with the normal neuroses of three generations trying to work out their problems together. The young person is busily engaged in finding out what life is like and who he is. He may make some false stabs, but in the process he makes important discoveries and becomes a person in his own right. To understand that he is trying to find a balance at three important points may make it easier to understand what is going on and what it means.

The first of the three points where balance is sought is between past and future. The young person seeks to extract from the past what he thinks he can use in building his future. That he may be inadequately prepared to judge what is valuable does not limit his effort to try. The more those who are closely related to him try to point out the inadequacy of his experience, the more he is determined to resist their judgment. For at the same time that he seeks a balance between past and future, he is also trying to find a balance between dependence and independence; to depend on parents at this point seems to violate his quest for his own essential being. And it may well be that youth has a point, for when we look at the world we are bequeathing to the next generation, we need not be proud. Because we are familiar with the cause-effect relationships that have produced the world we live in, we find it easier to accept it, with all its horrors. But a youth coming into this world, and seeing it as it is, cannot be expected to look to those who have created it for guidance in making a better one. It is at this point that a serious question is raised about the function of religion in society. If the church is so significant for life, youth asks, why has it not produced better fruit in the affairs of men? They may look elsewhere for answers. It is a wise pastor who interprets without defending, and who looks to the future for results rather than to the past. Youth can see the vision of a better world, for they have a great stake in it, but they want to take only from the past what they think can contribute to it.

The young person is also seeking a balanced self. He is aware of contending forces that move him one way or another. He wants to be sure of himself, but he is not certain which self he wants to be sure of. There is the self that judges and the self that is judged. There is the self that seeks to live by high ideals and the self that says it isn't worth the trouble. There is the religious self and the self that does not care about the church or any part of it. These selves are in contest with each other. The chance to win the loyalty of the finest self for a life-long commitment comes at this time in life. But it cannot be done by an appeal to outworn modes of thought or dated emotions. It can come through helping youth to get a perspective on himself, so he can better understand who and what he wants to become.

The third point at which balance is sought is in the relationship of dependence to independence. He cannot establish the limits of his own person if he is a subservient being. He must experiment with the boundaries of thought and behavior. He begins with his parents, who have made many of the decisions of life for him in the past. If he has been guided to accept more and more responsibility for his own behavior, this transition can come gradually and painlessly. But if his parents feel threatened by every show of independence on his part, he may have to assert himself in ways that are painful to him and difficult for them to accept. In his efforts to break with parental authority, he may feel uncomfortable and threatened himself. He may do things and then feel sorry for having done them, but also unable to express his feelings of remorse. At such times he may seek another adult in whom he can confide, and with whom he can share the growing edge of his life. A pastor often stands as a parent figure, but one removed from the emotional crises of home life. The chance to talk over the meaning of his behavior and his relationships with his parents can be useful for all concerned.

To live with and understand this period of growth takes a great deal of patience and grace. One day a youth who had taken an interim job as custodian of church property, in order to earn money for college, showed some resentment at pastoral supervision of his work. With a bit of good humor, he flexed his muscles and took a playful jab at the end of my nose. It was his intent to have his fist fall short of my nose by an inch or so. It gave him some inner satisfaction to see an adult flinch at such a motion. But evidently his arm had grown an inch or so since the last time he had done it, or he misjudged the distance. He connected sharply with the end of my nose and I saw stars for a moment. My first impulse was to retaliate in kind, but I thought better of it, for I was aware that he felt sorry about what had happened. So I said nothing and nursed my sore nose in silence. Eight years later he asked me to be the elder to share in the laying on of hands at his ordination. I wondered what might have happened to his career had I let my first impulse reign. The little things of life loom large to the youth, and the willingness of an adult to understand and be patient often bears good fruit where least expected.

The pastor, as a friend of youth, can help to bridge some of the gaps that develop between parents and their children. Sometimes this may be done in a pastoral counseling relationship with the family. Or sometimes the pastor has to step in as the champion of youth in order to protect them from the misunderstanding of parents who are overwrought by behavior that is hard to condone. Parents have even come to me with the complaint that their adolescent children must be insane, and needed to be committed to an institution to protect them against their behavior. At such times it is necessary to try to interpret the internal state of the youth so that the parents can understand that they have not spawned a monster, but rather are going through a difficult period with a youth testing himself, as well as others, in a growth process. It usually reassures parents to know that they are not alone with such problems, and that forbearance for a period will see it through. There are times when such counsel prevents actions that would be quite unfortunate for all concerned.

In some instances the small group process can be employed to bring parents of adolescents together for shared insight, information about what to expect of adolescent behavior, and how best to deal with it. This can best be done in the period just before the problems begin to develop.

It is also well to try to interpret parents to youth, for one of the important discoveries of the maturing process is to realize that parents are also people.

Many people and large amounts of money are needed to put a man in orbit. It calls for patient effort on the part of those who are not going anywhere to prepare the thrust that gets a person off the earth. To get a young person launched into a healthy and useful orbit in life calls for the patience and understanding of a sizable ground crew. Of these, the pastor is not the least, for he believes in growth and he wants the venture to be successful. He stands ready to make his contribution to the launching procedures. And the satisfaction that comes from watching the successful careers of the young people he has helped is one of the greater satisfactions of the ministry.

7

PASTORAL CARE OF PERSONS
IN THE MIDDLE YEARS

*B*ROADWAY PLAYS have spoofed the problems of the middle-aged. Novelists have built interesting plots around the characters who desparately fight the march of time and the waning of passion. Students of personality are concerned with the problems of those who run out of steam just at the time when life makes its greatest demands of them.

In the intimacy of the parish ministry, all of these hazards come alive with personal poignancy.

The laboratory for practical living that is each parish forces upon the pastor the most complicated problems, and among the middle-aged the conflicts between responsibility and irresponsibility, strength and weakness, vision and blindness are most acute. In the middle years the person is assumed to be at the height of his powers mentally, physically and emotionally. His competence has been tested, and his chance to verify his values has been exercised. Yet during these years the cumulative stress of anxiety, overwork and frustration can break an individual who has neglected his own inner resources and has taken his strength for granted.

Because of the leadership patterns in both church and community, many of those staggered by acute personal problems also happen to be leaders in the parish and the larger social group. Their behavior cannot be attributed to the inexperience of youth or to the vagaries of old age. Critical social and moral judgments are most ruthlessly applied to those in the middle years, and yet their needs and their problems call the more for understanding and perceptive treatment. How can the pastor and the program of the parish serve the needs of its middle aged members?

Let us look first at some of the typical crises that develop in the lives of persons from thirty-five to sixty. This is the quarter century within which success or failure becomes apparent. It is the time when the dreams one has set and the goals that have been visioned are reached or compromised. This is the time when the fear of age and the failure of feelings stirs emotions into irrational action.This is the time when the problems of parenthood reach their climax, when the brutal facts of unwise marriage choices can not easily be ignored. This is the time when a feeble philosophy of life produces its fruits of emotional inadequacy and triviality of action.

How do these problems look when they get up and walk around in live people?

*   *   *

Brenda had been a vivacious, self-reliant and independent person, successful at college and determined to have a career. She got a good job as editorial assistant on a national magazine. For ten years she lived a wonderful life, traveling, meeting interesting people, and enjoying the social whirl of a large city. At thirty-five she began to be uneasy. By the time she was thirty-eight she was deeply dissatisfied with life. Gradually her friends had married and developed other interests. She was left with a group of dead-beats and ne'er-do-wells for companions. She found herself alone more and more, with her apartment becoming a prison rather than a haven of peace in her busy world. She was invited to visit old friends, yet their activities with children and household tasks created irritation and resentment. When she tried to work harder she became tired, and visited the doctor often with a variety of minor complaints that were the physical expression of her generalized distress with life. One day amidst sobs that shook her whole body she summed up her plight saying, "What have I done? Am

I boxed in for good? I have no life that matters. Oh, what I would give to have someone who cared when or if I got home at night. Oh, just to have a baby of my own to hold tight. I have everything I wanted once, and now it is nothing to me. I slammed all the doors on life and now I can't get them open. What will happen to me?"

* * *

It was nearly midnight when Merritt S. called his pastor. He was a highly competent neurosurgeon, wealthy enough to retire at forty-five, and apparently well balanced and in love with his work. He asked to see the pastor at once on a most urgent matter. When he arrived at the pastor's study he slumped into an easy chair, shaking with anxiety, saying, "I don't know where to begin. I don't even know what is the matter." After a long pause, he continued, "I have to operate in the morning, but I don't think I can do it. I've lost confidence in myself." During another long pause he sat with his head buried in his hands. "Nothing like this has ever happened to me before. I'm frightened. I can't talk to anyone about how I feel. I can't let my patients find out. I know what my colleagues would say. I hate these psychiatric boys with all their theories. If I were my own patient I would send myself to a neurologist, but no—I can't. I know what he would say. . . . When the last patient left my office tonight I started walking—I wore a groove in the carpet in my waiting room. Then I called you. What am I going to do?"

For more that two hours the minister and the physician talked of work and stress and resources. Merritt talked out thought and feelings, made articulate anxieties that had long gone unspoken, gave vent to apprehensions about himself, his work, his way of life. Obviously more relaxed he breathed deeply, stretched himself and said, "I'd better be going. I feel better now. Wheel in the customers, sharpen up the knife. I'm ready to go to work." Next morning he called the pastor and said, "It went well. I was as good as ever." The pastor said, "Come and see me more often." About once a month Merritt calls his pastor and visits him to talk about anything and everything. He can talk with his colleagues about technical matters, but with his pastor he talks about his thoughts and feelings, his philosophy of life and his religious resources. He lets his fancy run free, and in this association of thought and feeling Merritt has found a way to deal with the stress that comes with overwork and the need for perspective. For years he thought this was unnecessary. Now he knows life is made up of more than work, medical journals and patients. He is taking account of himself as a person, and he is enjoying it.

* * *

Barbara S. was a leader not only in local church activities but also in the district's women's organization. When she spoke she did so with authority, and her ideas were so good and so well expressed that she gained a reputation as a competent executive and as a spiritually endowed person. One day she visited the pastor's study ostensibly to talk over a matter of church program. She paused in the middle of a sentence and said, "Have you noticed anything unusual about me lately?" Cautious in his response, the pastor said, "How do you mean?"

She answered explosively. "I never knew the menopause would be like this! I was the one who always laughed at the girls and their sad stories, but its actually worse than they ever said. Some days I think I'm going stark, raving mad. I'm so touchy I'm not fit to live with. I'm a mean, spiteful, vicious person, and the worst thing about it is I know it and can't do a thing about it. I'm just overcome by feelings I can't handle. I say things that I'm ashamed of. I do things that are frightful when I think about them. I hate myself for it. I even think I would be better off dead. You know, I even sometimes think of helping the process along. I look at the sleeping pills and say to myself, I say, 'Everybody would be better off without you around. You're no good to anyone. It would be better to be dead than to live in such a miserable state.' Is there anything that can be done for a miserable creature like me?"

* * *

Charles F. was a dignified, competent senior executive of his company. He had always been an ideal family man with joy in his children—and now in his grandchildren. In his middle fifties, he could be considered the symbol of success and stability. When he went to see his pastor he was fidgety and nervous. He sat down uneasily and looked around as if to check the room for microphones and look-through mirrors. He started the conversation by saying, "I have a problem, a very serious problem. In fact I would say I am in real trouble. I am desperate. I don't know which way to turn or what to do." Then he looked searchingly at the pastor and said, "I suppose you want all the gruesome details." The pastor responded, "No, I am not primarily concerned with 'gruesome details' as you call them. But if we are to think together about what is troubling you, we will have to share the main outline of the problem, at least." After quite a pause, Charles F. took a deep breath and said, "You may not believe this, but it's a woman. My secretary, in fact. She's worked for me for many years, and there was never any question about our relationship. She's in her late thirties. We have talked over thoughts and problems many times during the last fifteen years, and it meant nothing. I needed her at some business conferences, we had dinner a few times, and just to be nice I arranged for a show. Well, there were some drinks, I went to her room, and you can get the picture. I can't explain why I did it, for it is completely foreign to my past life. Well, to sum up, it has gone on like this for several months. I would like to break off but she becomes highly emotional. Now look—she is a fine person. She says she won't expose me or do any damage. She says she loves me and always has and can't live without me. She says if I break off she will quietly go away and take a lethal dose of sleeping pills. Naturally I don't want that to happen. I feel so guilty. I know I did wrong. I am afraid things will break out into the open. I have even thought of running away, taking my own life, trying to escape, but everything I think of creates more problems than it solves. So much is at stake in every direction. All I ever stood for is in the balance, my work, my family, my life. And I don't know what to do. I don't know what to do."

* * *

Mrs. Warren G. called the pastor's study in a state of agitation, wanting a conference at once. Her pastor arranged to see her. She burst into the study and almost before she was seated she was in deep sobs. When she was able to talk she said, "It's my son, Harold. We've got to do something about him at once. It's a long story but I thought we could handle it. Now I am at the end of my endurance. Every time I look at him I want to shriek. He is deliberately trying to drive me crazy. And he is succeeding!" The pastor inquired about Harold, a high school senior. He had observed the boy in youth groups and summer camp—good-natured, large, athletic, and yet so basically shy that his efforts to show-off were usually inept. Mrs. G. was a domineering former school teacher who treated everyone as a child and could not tolerate any questioning of her judgment on any subject. Mrs. G. went into great detail about her son's behavior, recounting his desire for a room of his own which he decorated with pictures of scantily-clad girls. She made much of his use of crude language. She said she thought she had reached the end when she smelled tobacco on his breath. But she went on in anguished fashion to point out that this had not been the end. She said he talked on the phone with other boys and said scandalous things about girls, "right in front of her." She said she took the phone away from him but he just called up again and said the same things louder than ever. And now the end had really come. This morning she had found three beer cans in his room, right out in the open. As she put it, "Here it was, right in my own house, where I've never allowed such a thing. I won't even allow my husband to take a drink. And now my son flaunts me and all I stand for, right under my own roof. Oh, how can I go on living like this with mutiny and such sinfulness in my own house? I have made up my mind. I am not going to let this go on another day. I called my husband on the phone at his office and told him we must take a firm stand. Harold must change or Harold must go. I will disown him before I stand by and watch him destroy himself and us. Warren said I should talk with you before I do anything. But I knew what you would say. I am right. I know it. I have no doubt. You agree with me, don't you? *Don't* you?"

* * *

Phyllis L. was bored to death, and this is not to use a cliché without meaning. It is a statement of fact. Oh, she hadn't had her rendezvous with the funeral director, but she was writing her own obituary day by day as she let a loss of interest in life waste her existence in small bits. Her husband worked long hours in his auto repair business, and was seldom at home. The children were grown, and the youngest was away at school. The small apartment where she lived required little housework and her husband acted as if he tried to stay away from home as much as possible. Phyllis puttered around, watched television until she knew all the "soap opera" characters, walked the block to the supermarket two or three times a week, and in between vegetated. She had few acquaintances, no friends, no interests, no real life. She had nothing to do and all the time in the world to do it. She did not come to her pastor to talk over her problem. One of her neighbors said to him, "Have you seen Mrs. L. lately? I know she isn't a member of our church, but whenever they need anything they call on us. I think she is in trouble. She's drinking a lot. Maybe you would want to stop and see her." When the pastor called, Phyllis L. yelled a husky, "Come in." She was sloppily dressed, unkempt in appearance, and quite obviously showing the effects of too much alchohol. When she saw the pastor she made an effort to get to her feet and uttered some remarks about her looks and the condition of the apartment. Without giving the pastor time to say a word she began to explain why she had not been to church and why it was difficult for her to get out. She then said she was not well and that the physician had ordered her to drink wine to keep relaxed. When she ran out of excuses and explanations of her condition, she complained of nosey neighbors and the trials of living in an apartment with such people. She drew in bold lines of a self-portrait of a person whose life has run out of meaning. In a vain effort to blot out emptiness she had just about obliterated her existence. And in the midst of her boredom and emptiness she did not grasp what was the matter.

* * *

The problem that often besets the middle-aged is compounded by the converging of many problems, each of which might be handled adequately. Yet when bunched together, they become overwhelming. The problems are usually the problems of normal people, but the hazards develop when there seem to be more problems than solutions.

The people we have looked at are not psychotic, and the neuroses they have developed may well be spoken of as the normal neuroses that come through circumstances rather than through acute personal inadequacy. They are the problems that come when parents, faced with the problems of involution, have to live through the stresses of adolescence with their children. They are the problems that develop when the pressures upon life are greater than the physical, emotional, and spiritual strength of the individuals involved. They are the problems of fatigue, failure, success, and a loss of perspective. They are the problems that emerge when life no longer proceeds on the momentum of youth, but must find its own meanings and purposes. They are the problems that spring up when a person begins to take stock of his life only to find that his goals have been elusive and the time of life is running out.

This is when questions begin to be asked about the ultimate meaning of all of the hustle and bustle and hard work, all the suffering and the sacrifice. Unless there are adequate answers available now, life may cave in, and the years that follow may be swallowed up in a misery of cynicism and despair.

In the face of these situations that afflict many of our middle aged persons, what have the pastor and the church to offer? They should be making an effort to do three things. First, they must be at work to give a preventative answer to many such problems before they develop. Second, they should be available for emergency aid when the problems do become acute. And third, they must offer a broad program for those in middle life that answers basic questions, provides healthful social life, and gives sustained spiritual nourishment.

The educational program for adults in the parish may well take into account the special needs of the middle years. The members may be acquainted with the nature and treatment of emotional response to glandular change, personal adaptation to changed social states, and spiritual resources for times of stress. The large numbers of widows in our culture are economically and socially induced, and it is important that persons be trained to think of life as a perpetual adjustment and death as a physical reality at the same time that it is a challenge to spiritual growth. It may well be that the preaching program of the church (which often has the best listening audience among the middle-aged) would direct its thought toward the actual problems that the middle-aged have to live with. At many points, from early years, people can be prepared for crises simply by being made aware of the fact that life is perpetual adjustment—and that competence in living is achieved not so much by gaining goals as by developing the inner strength to set worthy purposes.

The competence of the pastor in helping his people meet the crises of life is never more rigidly put to the test than in meeting the needs of the middle-aged. The counselor must realize that analytic techniques are no longer generally acceptable, because the personality structure has about it a rigidity that develops from long practice. The middle-aged person will be essentially the person he has always been and his problems must be met within that context. However, the counselor needs special skills both in understanding what the problems really are and also in wisely counseling in relation to them. The adult may have developed defense mechanisms through long practice that make it difficult for him to face himself. It is at this point that the group counseling process can be valuable, since in it a person sees his own problems in the lives of others, and is freed from his own need to employ defenses. Also the counselor needs to know that he is obliged to give short-term emergency aid to acute breakdowns, depressions and feelings of despair in facing failures. Parental failures, marriage failures, financial failures as well as spiritual failures call not so much for a complete rebuilding of life as they do for a skillful quest for the resources of the personality already existent. Resources that can be used for the immediate tasks of redirecting energy and rebuilding goals.

As far as the total program of the church is concerned, it should not be a place of frenzied activity, where people are forced by artificial stimulation to overwork their strength for false or imagined goals, but rather it should be a place of relaxed maturity where persons understand each other's needs, and work toward the resolution of them in tolerance and patience. The goals of achievement in the life of the church might often be re-examined in the light of the needs *of its members*—so that they are not being judged by their ability to meet certain personal goals of the pastor, but rather will be helped to seek meanings adequate for the needs of their own lives. And during this effort they must feel that the pastor as a person and that the church as an organization are working together to help them achieve the deeper satisfactions of their own selfhood.

When this is done, the middle-aged may be helped to keep on growing mentally and spiritually through the critical middle years into a sound and healthy state of being prepared not only for the older years, but also for eternity.

8

PASTORAL CARE OF THE AGED

*T*HE NUMBER of aged persons in our culture is increasing rapidly, posing individual and group economic, social and spiritual problems. The family frequently does not know how to care for its aged members while still preserving its own integrity. The older person may feel in the way, unwanted and unable to pay his share. In this picture of personal and social stress there is a pastoral ministry to perform.

Until recently there has been little careful study of the aging process. It is important for us to understand what happens in aging if we are to minister wisely to the older person. Generally speaking, older people have a difficult time. Dr. Martin Gumpert says, "The majority of people over the age of sixty-five lead an unhappy and frustrated existence today because they are pushed into a corner, remote from the stream of life, and are offered charity, pity and hobbies instead of dignified participation in gainful work." In his study, "Age and Achievement," Harvey C. Lehman makes it clear that the most creative age is in the fourth decade of life, but that in many skills and professions this productivity continues well into the eighth decade.

The passage of time has different effects on different people. What we usually speak of as aging is governed by at least four major factors and by a number of minor ones. Aging is subject to natural laws; the cycle of birth, growth, withering, and death is observed in nature in one form or another in all forms of matter. It may be millions of years before the atom of radium ages into an atom of lead, or it may be a few hours of a day in which the fragile moth leaves the cocoon, lays its eggs and dies. The natural process of organic response to the passing of time is everywhere observable. Man does not escape the basic laws of life to which he is subject along with the rest of nature.

But in man there are other forces at work to hasten or retard the process. People living in the same climate, eating much the same food, and participating in the same life processes have varying rates of physical aging. As Dr. Cecil G. Sheps has made clear, "Aging and disease are different processes. From the biological point-of-view, aging is a natural condition. It starts before birth at the moment of conception and goes on throughout life."* Even within one person there are varying rates of aging. Some cells in the nervous system last the lifetime of the individual; others are replaced every three or four days. No individual is of the same biologic age throughout. A person may have a cardio-vascular system equivalent to the average of forty-year-olds and a digestive system characteristic of sixty-five-year-olds.

No one knows what the prime of life is. Sprint records are usually made by runners in their twenties, but the marathon races are won by men around forty. Age involves changes, varied abilities, important compensations, and valuable experiences.

"As muscular vigor and speed decreases, coordinating skills often increase," says Dr. Sheps. "Aging reduces the tolerance of some persons to drugs, and increases that of others. Nutritional needs also change. There is, for example, a reduction of caloric requirements but an increased need for calcium and protein. Even the types of disease vary with age. Young persons tend to suffer from acute diseases while the aged are afflicted with chronic disease. And the

* Except where otherwise indicated, all references in this chapter are from statements by Dr. Sheps, lecturer on preventive medicine at Harvard University, and are quoted from "The New Frontiers of Aging," edited by Wilma Donahue and Clark Tibbitts, published by the University of Michigan Press.

causes of death change from generation to generation, depending on environment.

"In 1900 the five leading causes of death were, in this order, pneumonia, tuberculosis, diarrhea, heart disease and kidney disease. Now they are heart disease, cancer, deaths by violence, apoplexy and kidney disease." In 1900, chronic illness was responsible for approximately half of the deaths. Now it is responsible for 60 per cent of all disability and for 80 per cent of the deaths."

So four-fifths of deaths today are the termination of long-standing chronic illness. This makes treatment difficult, for diagnosis is approached with limited understanding.

"The disease is often considerably advanced before symptoms occur, thus making for delay in discovery and diagnosis," Dr. Sheps points out. "In youth, the course of disease is usually acute, self-limited, brief, immunizing, with little individual variation. In senescence, the cause is usually chronic rather than immunizing; it often produces increased vulnerability to other diseases. It is progressive and there is very wide individual variation. This produces long-lasting disability prior to death. As a matter of fact, we are particularly bad in combatting the so-called degenerative diseases among males over the age of forty-five, and also accidents among both sexes."

What we know about the physiological details of aging is surrounded by the ocean of our ignorance. "There is far too little research on the whole man—his individual psychology and its reaction to the way he lives his life—in relation to his future cardiac health or disease," Dr. Sheps comments. "Before heart disease is discoverable, individuals can differ in their mode of life and in every morphological, biochemical, physiological and social characteristic we can measure. It is reasonable to expect that these individual differences in the healthy state are related to great differences in the eventual appearance of, freedom from, heart disease. . . . Prevention must be the keynote and hope, but so far there is extremely little to offer because almost nothing is known of the pre-disease personal characteristics, of the life-long habits of diet, of exercise, of emotion, of physical and social environment, of other illnesses and accidents far removed in time, which make one man a candidate for early death and give his fellow man relative immunity."

The evidence accumulates that all of life is involved in the nature and behavior of the aged, that what we have been all our life goes far to determine what we will be like when we are old.

While certain types of physical disability appear to increase with the aging process, many older people enjoy excellent health. The natural progression of life does not necessarily carry with it the aches, pains and groans that many acquire. Our knowledge of the physiological aspects of aging gives us but slight clues as to what happens to the whole man with the passing of time.

An important social factor must be considered in the behavior of the aging. In some Mediterranean countries the useful role of women is considered to be over when the children reach maturity. Many women accept the idea that they are old at forty and look and act as they picture themselves to be. Women in a different culture adopt the ideas and attitudes of their surroundings and so retard the evidences of the aging process.

This social manifestation is observed in reactions to retirement. Many people live full and useful lives until the time of retirement, and then deteriorate rapidly. It has been noted that many people die within six months of retirement. The feeling that they do not serve a socially useful function, plus the fact that they have no sustaining routine or interest, causes their lives to fall apart. Yet people whose retirement is a prelude to another interesting and useful phase of living go on for years enjoying health and well being.

Many of the physical indispositions of the aged appear to be not so much physical disorganization as social and psychological disintegration. This is borne out by research on the mental health of the aged. It has been an easy practice to attribute signs of disintegration among the aged to arteriosclerotic brain disease or to so-called senile dementia. The symptoms that often lead to a diagnosis of physiological breakdown may not be these, however, but may result from loss of interest in life and a gradual withdrawal from meaningful living. "Competent investigators have demonstrated . . . that either of the two clinical diagnoses is often not confirmed by post-mortem gross or microscopic examination of the brain," declares Dr. Sheps.

While there has been little coordinated research into the nature of personality response to the aging process, there is much evidence to sustain the idea that aging can be retarded by favorable conditions of mind and environment. A physician told me of two hypochondriacal sisters who had long harassed him with their imagined ailments. One day, almost facetiously, he asked, "Why don't you two learn Spanish? It would be good for you." Accepting this with the authority of a prescription, they did, and started a new era in their lives with new friends, new experiences and travel in Latin countries. Their ailments disappeared and they enjoyed the best years of their lives, physically, mentally and emotionally. And that's not a particularly uncommon occurrence.

It may also work the other way. The increase in alcoholism among the aged is another form of escape from the boredom that often comes with retirement.

Much of what happens to people with the passing of years is a product of a number of interrelated conditions. Proper diet and stimulating living conditions, a healthy philosophy of life and a creative attitude of mind can do much to give health and vitality to the older years. The absence of such advantageous conditions may hasten deterioration of body, mind and spirit. More than we have ever dared to think, the advancing years can be made spiritually productive in such a way that all of life is made more satisfying. Aging is not so much a measurement of the passing of time as it is a loss of some vital, spiritual capacity that values life.

The attitude toward the older person in any given society appears to have a definite bearing on the health and well being of its older members. The way one looks at his own life is also important. The person who thinks he is old is apt to be. The person who thinks young, who enjoys new interests and young ideas, keeps something of eternal youth about him.

Though the aging process may have some bearing on the

general health of the individual, there are no diseases that appear to afflict only the aged. There are no limits to the good health and joy of living that can be shared by older people if the internal and external conditions sustain it. And no one need die of disease. All may die healthy. Dying may be the fitting end of a natural process where the person who has fruitfully completed his span of years may "wrap the draperies of his couch about him and lie down to pleasant dreams."

Science is doing strange things with the theory of time. It no longer views time as an abstract dimension to suit the convenience of men's minds, but rather as an imponderable dimension of the creative process. The creative mind seems able to dart in and out of time. The phenomenon of precognition gives substance to the conjecture that some power has mastery even over time. If this is true of mental activity of a limited type, we may foresee the time when disciplined minds may even "take a tuck in time" and find the quality of being that Ponce DeLeon sought so persistently. It may well be that the surmising soul is reaching out toward a state of being where the creative power of the mind is master of those measurements long considered to exist only for its convenience.

As science becomes more adept in dealing with those aspects of existence that are less materialistic and more akin to the spiritual, it may give further verification to the philosophical judgment of Santayana who said, "Nothing is inherently and invincibly young except spirit. And spirit can enter a human being perhaps better in the quiet of old age and dwell there more undisturbed than in the turmoil of adventure." Perhaps the only question one would ask in response to such a statement is, "Who better than Santayana knew the meaning of spiritual adventure?"

In a home for the aged, researchers asked residents whether they considered themselves old or not. Those who did not think they were old were more intact physically and psychologically than those who identified themselves as old. Those who held a young opinion of themselves had more hope than despair, more love than indifference and more real motivation. The pastoral ministry to the aged should help create an image of a self filled with vitality employed in a life worth living.

The creation of this image must be started long before the years arrive when interest might be lost. Things happen to people as they expect them to happen. Expectancy of a good and rich life equips a person to deal with whatever comes with courage and competence. All that we can learn of the physical conditions that affect aging indicates that the major factor is not organic but psychological. The things that happen to the body are indications of what is happening in the mind and emotion of the individual. Weariness and despair stimulate the aging process while interest and strong motivation for life delay it.

Older people in the church need to feel that there is something that satisfies their deeper needs for living. The qualities that Santayana speaks of are perhaps best set at work in those who have time for meditation and contemplation. The prayer life of the parish can be enriched by its more mature members. Often these people have not taken the time to cultivate their spiritual natures during the busier years of life; they come to the years when they do have time, anxious to grow spiritually. The program of activities for older members should not be designed merely to use up time, but rather to give a growing edge to life. Spiritual exploration— a chance to ask important questions and an impulse to reach an understanding of the spiritual life in all its dimensions— should be encouraged during these years.

Many of the important tasks of the church can be done by people who have time on their hands. Committee assignments may be made with these people in mind. The older person wants to remain useful, able to do things for others. He becomes uncomfortable when he feels that people are showing him special deference because of his years. He not only resists such attentions but actually resents them. While it is wise to recognize that certain activities must be limited with the passing of time, why not assume that when one door closes another can be opened?

The pastor's role with the older members of the parish is quite different from his ministry to the shut-ins. He is not seeking to minister to those who passively accept a retired role, but to those who are seeking creative ways to use the time retirement makes available. Activity, interest, enjoyment, usefulness, and spiritual growth are the key words of such a pastoral interest.

It may be wise to have some group activities where people associate on the basis of their age, but it is more important to have groups with mixed ages so that some of the values of the old family constellation can be preserved. It is well known that stability and perspective are transmitted through the family group that has depth as far as age is concerned.

The old rural family set-up always had some of three generations present. All had their work to do and each could learn from the other. This developed tolerance and good will, and made it possible to dissipate emotional tensions in a broad family pattern. Children did not always have to endure the judgments of parents but could turn to grandparents and uncles or aunts. The older members could enjoy the life-stimulating activities of children. The natural pattern of life cycles was clearly shown in this rural pattern. Much of that has been lost in the small family unit of modern urban life, and if the benefits of it are to be preserved it may well be in the groups of different ages that meet within the church to share and grow in interest and good will. Morning services of worship have always had this quality.

It would be unfortunate if the aged were considered as a handicapped group, to be supplied with amusement, pink teas and boring displays of slide collections (whose owners can find no one else upon whom to inflict them). The aged members should share in all activities with all of the vigor and enthusiasm of spiritually endowed persons, rich in their capacity to contribute and important in the role they can play.

After we have learned all we can about the aging process, we should back off and look at ourselves. Every day we are getting older, and the time will come when we may ourselves be considered among the aged. But we will be the same persons with the same background and interests. We will bring to our later years all that we have invested in life. The wisely invested present is essential to the richly endowed future, and that is true for every age. The whole program of the church can help people prepare for life, and this life is indivisible. It is to be enjoyed here and hereafter.

The pastor who grows with his people will keep them growing with him. And though the years may pile up, none will ever really become old.

9

PARISH-CENTERED COUNSELING

*T*HE PASTOR'S ROLE is never a simple one. He plays many roles, and some of them seem to be contradictory. He is preacher, prophet, spiritual adviser, organizational leader, group participant, and friend.

And in recent years, new demands have been placed

131

upon the pastor as a counselor. This was a role he had always assumed in an informal way, as the study of the care of souls in the history of the church verifies. But now he is expected to function in a more formal way. Millions of people who saw military service were advised to talk their problems over with the chaplain. Other millions read articles in popular magazines and in the columns of professional advisers urging them to relieve their mental and emotional stress by talking problems over with their pastors. This increasing demand created a problem for the pastor-counselor, for if he were sensitive to the deeper needs of people, he felt his inadequacy; and if he were not sensitive, he failed to meet the emotional needs of the counselee.

Those concerned with the training of pastors sought to find a philosophy and technique for counseling. An exploration of various philosophies of personality led to a variety of interpretations and practices. The Freudian insight into the nature of human personality made men aware of depths of being that had not been considered before. The importance of lower levels of consciousness in determining behavior was emphasized. While this was significant, the Freudian concept of motivation, with its pessimistic view of human nature, does not lend itself to pastoral needs. Rank and Jung broke with their teacher, Freud, at the point of motivation and gave a broader basis for interpreting human behavior, with regard to both motivation and the nature of the human psyche. The writings of Sullivan and Fromm emphasized the social context of behavior. Clara Thompson and Karen Horney developed therapeutic concepts built on the basic healthy drives that move individuals toward resolving inner conflicts.

Perhaps the most useful counseling resource for those working in the field of the pastoral ministry has come from Carl Rogers. His optimistic concept of human nature, and his techniques for stimulating the creative endowment within the individual, lend themselves to goals that are more traditionally within the religious framework. More recently Jerome Frank, with his emphasis on group forces and his skepticism about the adequacy of any of the so-called psychotherapeutic schools, has directed thought toward the constructive forces at work not only within the individual but also within the inspirational and persuasive groups that are a part of his environment.

Each of these students of personality, and many more that connot be mentioned in this brief chapter, have made contributions to the growing body of theory and practice that is the basis of modern insight into pastoral counseling. Because no one school or philosophy has an adequate concept of human personality from the Christian point of view, it is essential to draw from varied sources and to develop an amalgamation which serves the purposes of the parish minister.

In practice, the approach to pastoral counseling has been marked by trial and error, and in its present state of development it seems unwise to champion any one process or method of procedure. In larger churches a staff ministry has made it possible for specialists to perform the varied roles of the ministry. However, this has not been entirely satisfactory because most people have a preconceived idea of the pastor's role which they bring with them into the relationship. The specialist in one phase of the ministry finds it difficult to adapt his specialty to the total demands of the parish. Also, relatively few churches can support that type of specialized ministry. Perhaps the solution will come in the more adequate training of all pastors in the varied demands that modern parish work requires.

But for the present the problem of adequate parish-centered counseling remains. Some men, carefully trained in a clinically oriented program, find themselves inadequately prepared for the scope of parish problems. Their techniques are not understood at the parish level, and they are apt to feel frustrated and even assume that they have failed through reasons that they cannot understand. In some instances they give up this phase of parish work and retreat into a liturgical emphasis, or take up teaching or an institutional chaplaincy where conditions are more favorable for their specialization. On the other hand, men with a theological emphasis that is pessimistic about human nature discount the values of counseling and ignore that aspect of the parish ministry.

The problem is not that simple, however. The nature of the parish ministry does not let a minister decide whether he will be a counselor; it merely gives him a chance to decide whether he will be a good or a poor one. The traditional role of the pastor in the parish invests him with an authority. This is shown in the privilege of the pulpit. He is expected to be an interpreter of life and its meaning. Few pastors are so insensitive or inaccessible that they are not involved in the human contacts that emerge from the life crises of their members. What they do and say, how they act and what they communicate verbally and nonverbally, has its impact on their people, and to that extent they are engaged in counseling.

The new role in which the pastor is cast by people who seek his guidance in their life crises gives him a chance to be useful, or, in effect, to reject them. If the pastor withdraws from contact with his people at such times, they are perplexed, he goes on the defensive, and the basic problem is compounded.

The solution seems to lie in a synthesis of the old role of the pastor, with all of the status that is invested in it by persons of the parish, and a new understanding of his opportunity to relate himself to the special needs of his people.

The pastor's counseling relationship with his people is somewhat different from the clinically-oriented and professionally-insulated relationship that the secular counselor has with his clients or patients. Like it or not, the pastor is inescapably bound up with an inherited tradition. The counselee comes to the pastor with some basic assumptions that cannot be ignored. He thinks of the pastor as a religious person. He thinks of him as a part of a tradition that values persons and wants to teach them a way of life. He thinks of a pastor as a person with clear ideas of what is right and wrong. He may come to the pastor because he feels the need of a moral judgment.

He also sees the pastor in a symbolic role, for he associates him with the other aspects of his ministry. In his struggle to be a responsible person, he turns to the pastor as a symbol of responsibility. In his struggle for maturity, he turns to the pastor as a symbol of maturity. In his struggle for a more adequate concept of being, he turns to his pastor as a symbol of true being and becoming. While none of these symbolic qualities are deliberately or actively claimed by the pastor, he has little control over the image his parishioners have of him. Yet he must be aware of it and responsive to it. It is a primary element in the pastoral counseling relationship.

This relationship has a dynamic quality before it begins, which may be an asset in the process. The pastor who says in effect, "When you come into my counseling room, forget that I am a pastor," is asking an unreasonable adjustment of his counselee. He is a pastor, and for good or ill he must use the mantle cast over his shoulders, for he cannot do otherwise. In the process of counseling he may go far to modify the image that is brought by the parishioner, but he cannot ignore that there is one, and that it differs considerably from the image that the average person has of a secular counselor.

Nor is the pastor ever separated from his organizational role. He is a churchman. He represents an institution that has a body of beliefs and practices. This, too, may be an asset, for many who come to him may unconsciously be seeking a group relationship. The church for them may be a security group, a unifying group, or a status group. In his role with the institution, the pastor is invested with certain clearly established characteristics. He is an authority. He is an interpreter. He is a competent adviser. But in his work with individuals outside the group, he must understand that many people have been injured by groups, and some group processes endanger and threaten the disordered person. On the other hand many needy people seek the support of a group as a step toward self-acceptance. And for all people there is a dimension of life that is never completely fulfilled apart from healthy group relationship.

The pastor cannot discount his group role or the preconceived ideas that the counselee has about him. Nevertheless, he can go far to create an atmosphere within which productive counseling can take place. Conversation is a personal encounter. He can use his skills as a listener to create a status in the mind and emotions of the counselee. A willing listener may be a new experience for the counselee. The act of listening to another with undivided attention is an act of loving acceptance. Being able to talk with one who is willing to listen leads to self-revelation. What is said takes on new meaning. One does not need to direct conversation in order to give it direction. An empathetic listener invites a process of identification which stimulates thought and feeling and which may lift communication to a level that the counselee had not experienced before. But the process of listening creatively does more than give status to the words that are said; it also gives meaning to words unsaid. The counselor should assure the parishioner that he needn't say anything he does not want to, but also that he should give special thought to what is difficult or impossible to verbalize, for these may be clues to the core of his problem. In this way even the things that are not said become meaningful. And the counselor, with his skill at reading between the lines, can make it easier for the counselee to take the next step toward self-revelation.

Sometimes the parishioner may want to give words to an idea or feeling, but, because of his preconceptions about the pastor's role, may hesitate to become explicit. At this point there may be need for reassurance and further affirmation of acceptance. A simple phrase such as, "Yes, I understand," or "I know how you must feel about that," may be sufficient. The nature of the communication and the feeling of rapport will indicate whether such assurance can be wisely used; the important thing is for the counselee to feel that he is talking to someone who is not remote or separated from him in his difficult process of self-revelation. What is happening to the counselee is of utmost importance. If the pastor feels defensive, insecure, or threatened, he will undoubtedly communicate this. If his primary concern is for the counselee, he will be less inclined to try to interpret in order to prove his own adequacy, and he will sustain the creative encounter with the growing edge of the personality who shares the conversation with him. His listening, when freely and skillfully done, is itself the best assurance of support, and a guide to the process.

The counselor must also realize that his listening is a responsibility, for from it he gets a clearer picture of what is going on in the mind and emotions of the counselee. While he may not want to admit that he is engaged in a diagnostic process, he cannot help it. Diagnosis is not merely a medical activity. The parishioner engaged in a form of self-diagnosis when he first decided he would talk with his pastor. The pastor is engaged in a practical form of diagnosis when he tries to determine whether his parishioner needs to be referred to a specialist for more skilled help. In listening the pastor is alert not only for what speech reveals but for what is not said. He is aware of the content of words, but also the deeper meanings that show through gestures and repetitions of words and phrases, as well as the general state of emotions as they are said. He listens for logical or illogical sequences of ideas. He makes special note of the non-sequitors, the points at which excessive emotion is displayed, and the violations of cause-effect thinking. He is alert to the symbols of disturbance, to the patterns called "syndromes." He senses when feelings are inapproriate, too little or too much. He is sensitive to the defenses of the parishioner as he reveals his inner struggle. As he is engaged in the skilled processes of listening, he is also engaged in determining whether there is a deep fissure in the personality, whether the behavior can be worked through at the conscious level, or whether his obligation to his parishioner requires that he consult with an expert in the field of human emotions about the problem.

While there appears to be no fixed rule for classifying people, there are some general behavior and thought patterns that can be used for practical diagnosis, and this should be one of the aspects of creative listening. In general, the person who is having active trouble with himself and his relations with others is showing neurotic manifestations; the person who is remote from the "feeling" aspect of his problem has built for himself an unreal world, and may be showing psychotic manifestations. The person who appears to be beyond any normal affective relationships may well be basically a sociopathic individual.

The relationship with the counselee, however, should not be overborne by the counselor's preoccupation with diagnosis. When the counselor decides that he can usefully engage in a counseling process, he has already made what amounts to a practical diagnosis. And many of those who come to him will not fall into any of the previously mentioned categories. They may be dealing with circumstantial problems, or asking for information, or responding to a stress that seems intolerable, and be seeking help in the crises of life that are so common to all of us.

In the history of the church there has always been a place for the spiritual guide. Recent literature from Europe shows an increased interest in pastoral care primarily as a form of spiritual guidance. While the counselor may use all the insights that come from specialized training in personality dynamics and counseling skills, he employs these for the special roles that the pastor can fulfill, roles not met adequately by other professional groups in our culture. The immediate question here is to guide or not to guide. Does the pastor violate the principles of good counseling if he assumes the role of the spiritual guide? Does he, in the light of his ordination and his special training, fall short of the meaning of his ministry if he does not meet the needs for spiritual guidance when they are clearly presented to him?

A hazard of the pastor's role is the authority granted him in spiritual matters. Without realizing it, he may engage in subtle intrusions on the personality of another, just when he is trying to avoid it. Yet in times of spiritual crises he may deny his parishioners what they seek most if he withholds direct suggestions or specific guidance in such matters. However, if he is sensitive to the movement of emotion in his counselees, and equally aware of the dangers of over-structuring his relationships with them, he can move wisely on a middle ground, fulfilling his ministry without denying the growth needs of his counselee.

Spiritual guidance may be a matter of information. A

psychiatrist who referred a patient to me said, "This is a matter of information. My patient is confused about religious matters. You can help her out at this point. You answer her questions, and I'll do the counseling." It was interesting to discover that her main questions were about the meaning of life, the nature of sin, and what could be done about feelings of real guilt. This could hardly be dealt with without engaging the emotions. Actually, it appeared that the psychiatric process had bogged down at the point of spiritual needs, and the information could not be communicated wisely without an understanding of the patient's other problems.

There are times when information, explanation, and interpretation are necessary to clear the way for the next stage of growth. If the pastor is aware of the larger context within which questions are asked, he can more adequately assume the special role of spiritual guidance. It is always well to remember that people often come with spiritual questions to get a foot in the door, only to reveal their more basic concerns with the passing of time. It is essential when giving this information to be sensitive to the emotions that surround the communication. At no point must the pastor ignore the legitimacy of the counselee's feelings, or deny the integrity of the feelings themselves, or fail to be aware of the deeper purposes for which guidance is sought.

The spiritual guide has a privileged role but also a hazardous one. Never is he more personally vulnerable than when he deals with the religious presuppositions of life. Here he is more apt to be talking about himself than his counselee's needs. Under the protection of a learned method and a carefully defined role, he feels safe. When he gets out into the deep waters of the spiritual and religious needs of others, he may be less inclined to accept the implication of their questions, for he may feel he has to defend his own ordination and way of life.

For this reason the religious counselor must learn a special discipline. He will utterly destroy his relationship with the counselee if he allows prejudice, projection, or aggression to creep into his relationship with the one whom he would help. The rights of the counselee remain, unqualifiedly, to be accepted, to be heard, to find satisfaction at the point where his growing interests warrant it.

So pastoral counseling is essentially a religious process. It is a quest for the ultimate meaning of life in one's own nature, and in the deep nature of others. The pastor cannot engage in these encounters without a point of focus beyond himself, and a cosmic purpose and design in his own life. The religious counselor operates on a different philosophy and with different presuppositions from the secular counselor. He thinks of man differently, and he cannot always hide this assumption. He is always an instrument of self-realization and self-fulfillment at this higher level. He wants it to show in healthy group awareness and relationship with others. He wants it to find expression, not in a crippling and life-destroying religious pattern, but rather in the achievement of mature religion. To this end he is committed to a school of thought, just as many secular therapists have their devoutly held ideas and their working faith. The counselor, within the framework of the church and the religious presuppositions about life, works to overcome resistence to this basic philosophy, to peel away the defenses in a slow and sensitive process, to encourage self-examination and analysis, but always with a concern that the counselee become the person God endowed him to be. This seems to put the religious counselor in an untenable position; the minister appears to be an instrument in a process that is dictated by the counselee at the very time the pastor champions a way of life that undergirds his conviction about the counselee, and is determining his role in relation to the development of the counselee's competence to deal with life. How can this dilemma be resolved?

The pastor-counselor finds his adequacy not in denial but in fulfillment of his special role. He gains his competence by employing the resources that are peculiarly his. A recent book of Carl Rogers, *On Becoming a Person,* may well be a launching pad from which he begins, but he does not end there. As Jerome Frank points out, the effectiveness of the therapeutic process is shrouded in mystery. No one is quite sure what inspires creative change in the individual; certainly, however, it is not inspired by an inadequate philosophy of man. Secular therapies seem to succeed in spite of inadequate philosophies, rather than because of them. The creative element seems to lie in the encounter with one who cares enough to give time and energy to help a person achieve selfhood, to become the person he needs and wants to be. The religious counselor has resources here that he has probably not fully appreciated or adequately used.

The religious counselor starts with a status that the secular counselor has difficulty in ever achieving. The pastor is endowed with a tradition of caring. He represents an institution that employs worship to inspire man's exalted view of himself. He works to interpret a way of life that has cosmic worth and significance. He can help one become not only a person in his own eyes, but also a being of worth in the sight of God.

The counselee presents himself, with his needs for self-acceptance, in an atmosphere that already has established the value of his being. He seeks it in a religious community, from a pastor who believes in man in order to help men to believe in themselves. Instead of denying any part of this endowment, he can work to bring it to its highest realization.

To this end the pastor can use all of the insights that have been developed in clinical settings, and combine them with the resources that are parochial. He can use all that has been developed through the sciences of personality as a basis for his concept of exalted human personality. He can use the group resources of the parish to give meaning to all that he has learned through the study of group dynamics and group therapeutics. He can employ the insights of scientific society to enhance a spiritual society that already believes in man, to help man to believe in himself. The controlled environment of the spiritual community then becomes an asset rather than a liability. The special role of the pastoral counseling relationship is supported by personal, group, and social resources that do not exist in any other privileged human context. It would be tragic indeed if these special resources were merely an appendage to a secular philosophy and a secularly imposed method. Rather, the special genius of the Christian tradition and view of man should use the insights of secular research and study and build a practice of its own, worthy of its special opportunity.

This young field of pastoral counseling must develop a challenging new concept of wholeness and healing that can offer leadership to related fields. Related professional studies reinforce the belief that the pastoral role has unique resources to be developed. To this goal we should direct our further study in the years ahead.

How might this best be done? We have learned much from the clinical training programs that deal primarily with clinical problems. The values of this intensive study have sharpened the tools of the pastoral ministry. But there needs to be a significant and intensive study of the unique resources of the parish-centered counseling ministry. Here the people are different. The differences, to be sure, are differences of relationship and not of personality structure, but they are significant enough to warrant detailed study.

Such a program should begin with the parish and its resources. It should develop its assumptions with a recognition of the varied role of the pastor-counselor. It should take into account the resources that the varied relationship affords. It could be worked out through practicums and in-training workshops, taught by those whose experience has been primarily in the parish. It could be supplemented by seminary training that puts as much emphasis on parish-oriented counseling as it does on institutional counseling. But such a program must recognize that the approach, the resources and the privileges are quite different.

The theological dimension for pastoral care would have to be emphasized in order to add the needed dimension to secular insight. The movement could then grow from resources to revelation, from competence in understanding personality dynamics to mediating God's redeeming love, from capacity to adjust to the power to become, and from the clinical to the cosmic.

The uniquely privileged role of the parish-centered counseling relationship, and the rich and unmined resources to be employed in that relationship, would then be developed, and pastoral counseling would more truly come into its own.

10

PASTORAL CARE OF THE
SPIRITUALLY INJURED

*T*HE PEOPLE who come to the pastor in the parish
usually make their initial approach on a religious problem. A woman may be concerned with feelings of jealousy,
or a man may be troubled about inadequacy, or parents may
feel threatened by their children and their behavior; yet

the problem is most often originally phrased in religious terms. The person says that he cannot pray, or has lost contact with God, or feels that he is really an atheist or an agnostic.

Such initial questions, as we have seen, may be but the point of entry into a variety of other problems. Sometimes the person does not know what is bothering him, and chooses a point of departure that he believes would be acceptable to the pastor. At other times he is not quite sure how the pastor will respond to his deeper needs, so he poses a religious question to test the pastor's response before going ahead with the problems that genuinely concern him. But in all such instances it is reasonable to assume that the person is suffering from a sore spot in his soul, a spiritual injury for which he seeks some help.

Mrs. L. expressed the fear that she had committed the unforgivable sin. She had had a breast removed because of a malignant growth. She said she felt that God was punishing her for having committed a sin beyond forgiving. Then she said she could not believe in a God who would do that to a person. Through several sessions she failed to say what she thought the sin might be, and it developed with time that she did not know what it might be either. She was baffled, confused and injured by what had happened to her. She needed help to go on living, but did not know what kind of help or really how to get it.

She appeared to be a depressed person who did not care much what happened to her; yet underneath all she said, she seemed to care tremendously. This woman showed the symptoms of deep spiritual injury, and the injury seemed to be at the point of her basic assumptions about life and her relationship with a cosmic order. She wanted a faith, but the beliefs she had been equipped with in early life were not strong or sure enough to carry her through her present state. A diffused resentment, anxiety and bitterness possessed her, and she was looking for a way of life that could carry her through the fears that had been triggered by the discovery of a malignant growth.

Sometimes the spiritually injured have lost faith in themselves. They may have had high hopes for life, they may have set goals for themselves that they have not realized, and with the rush of the years feel that they can never become what they wanted to be. Sometimes they are troubled by the problems of parenthood. They want to love their children but feel threatened by them. Sometimes they have become involved in behavior that shatters their self-image; they want help in building again a foundation for life adequate for true self-esteem.

More often than we realize the problem *is* essentially spiritual. In the stresses of life, they have outgrown the puny concept of God taught them in church school, and feel guilt at rejecting the idea. The cozy little universe that could be manipulated by magical religious practice is gone, and they have nothing to put in its place. They fear they have become atheists. Life has injured them and they reject the old ideas in anger. In turn, they feel rejected by a cosmic order that seems to have denied them what had once been promised. Be a good person and God will be good to you, was the original bargain. But the goodness of God has not been apparent; now they must decide whether to reject God or to assume the burden of guilt for not being the type of person that God would reward. This delayed stage of religious growth may be painful but it represents an opportunity for the pastor. If he denies the problem and brushes it aside by preaching part of a left-over sermon, or coming to God's defense, he is missing the opportunity. Rather, it is a time to find out what is really going on in the depths of being, so that normal, healthy growth can be started again.

Usually the fear of being an atheiest grows from a rejection in some past experience. The concept of God as a personalized Father may have been injured by unhappy child-parent relationships; only with the passing of time and new crises has the problem become explicit. Usually a breakdown in multiple relationships, and the fears associated with this breakdown, motivate one to make the break explicit at the point where it seems safest. In effect the person is saying, "I have found that my philosophy of life is inadequate and I am looking for another."

Sometimes the subject is approached more tentatively; the person says he feels he is becoming an agnostic because he can no longer be sure of what he believes or whether he believes in anything. This may well be his way of saying that he has lost faith in himself and so finds it difficult to have faith in anything else. Or his small structure of religious belief may have been shattered by insights of science and experience. He finds it impossible to go back to the old ways of thinking and he has not yet gained the courage to build a new and more adequate philosophy of life. New values are needed, and the approach to the pastor is a cry for help.

If the pastor is concerned primarily with the religious problem, he will probably miss the chance to be helpful. If the pastor feels threatened by an expression of disbelief, he may feel impelled to come to the defense of God. This further assaults the injured person and his second state is worse than his first. Actually the fact that he is there is evidence of his belief that God is love and will understand his emotional plight. The pastor should do the same. What is being revealed by the individual is more apt to be an expression of doubt in himself, a lack of worth, and a need for a broadening of the foundations of life so that he can get on with the tasks of living. It is important to accept the verbal expressions so that the deeper needs of the individual can be judged.

Sometimes the problems are dramatized in obsessive-compulsive behavior. The alcoholic usually comes under this heading. He is having trouble with life. Under stress he seeks help through "self-applied psychotherapy." He wants to get away from the pain. The molecular structure of chloroform, ether and alcohol are much the same, and the anaesthetic effects are the same. Because the two former substances are inhaled, the effect may be lethal, but alcohol is somewhat safer to use because it is absorbed through the tissues of the alimentary canal. Generally before the person can take a lethal dose, he is unable to administer any more of it to himself. But he has indicated what he feels is his need. It is to get away from what plagues him.

Usually the alcoholic feels competent to handle his own

therapy up to a certain point. Then he may admit his help-lessness and seek aid. Admonition and sermonizing are futile, for the alcoholic is already overburdened with re-morse; but resources to sustain him in a quest for sobriety can come from outside. The obsessive-compulsive person can substitute one interest for another. His interest in re-ligion or in Alcoholics Anonymous may sustain him under stress just as his former use of alcohol appeared to do. His problem may be deeply rooted in dependency needs and emotional inadequacy for life. The pastor who is helpful to the compulsive person must identify with the individual and walk with him through the valley of the shadow, not as a judge but as a friend who understands and is willing to share the struggle for a new way of life. The essential na-ture of the compulsive person is that of energy vigorously expended in destructive directions. The same energy can be used creatively and a spiritually injured person can stop injuring himself when he finds a way to use his energy wisely and well. The religious counselor can help to inspire new directions and help to make the creative venture worth the effort.

Often the spiritually injured person is suffering from depression. This dark and frightful mood makes life an un-happy prospect. Each new day dawns with apprehension and night comes with the prospect of tortured sleep. The mood is cumulative, and the more one is depressed, the more there seems to be to cause depression. This is char-acterized by turning anger against the self. Things go wrong, the person blames himself. From this guilt comes increased self-judgment with an accumulation of anger for which there seems to be no outlet. The body chemistry is affected by the mood and so the downward cycle continues as the body chemistry further stimulates the mood. This is why the depressed person often has a gray look, for the physiological processes are actually slowed down by the mood. If he is careless in appearance, it is because nothing seems to matter.

Sometimes the guilt is real and can be dealt with by constructive action. Sometimes the guilt is imagined, related to inner fears of rejection that may have had their inception early in life. Here the pastor may serve as a safe channel through which anger can be expressed, for often the anger is against cosmic forces. As the symbol of cosmic relationships, the pastor may be a useful object for such anger.

At other times the pastor may give the assurance of forgiveness so that through confession and restitution, the burden may be lifted. At the same time he may prescribe (and even share in) certain basic physical actions to stimulate increased bodily and glandular function so that the downward cycle of behavior may be reversed. Merely taking a long walk with a depressed person may help to change the mood. It is not productive to try to argue a person out of this state of mind, for he is usually not approachable at that level. But the attitudes and activities that can help him again to accept himself and gain some new meanings for his existence are important.

There are also religious roots for the paranoid state. The person who loses faith in himself soon begins to project his basic attitude of mind outward toward others. He becomes suspicious and thinks others are trying to do to him what he might subconsciously like to do to himself. Such persons may function quite well in many areas of life and have difficulty in a limited relationship or type of activity. Some may use their emotional states in productive fashion and in so doing protect themselves from the full impact of their emotional state. They make good detectives or private investigators. Often they make hobbies of weapons of aggression and become gun collectors. Unconsciously they are building up security against what they feel are the intentions of others.

This type of person is a trouble maker in group activities, always being aggressive as a form of defense. Just as the depressed person has lost hope, so the paranoid has lost faith. Nothing should be done to enhance his suspicion or to further injure his faith, and in instances where his behavior becomes threatening, he should be referred for special treatment, since his loss of faith tends to make him inaccessible to the more normal means of approach.

People who show their spiritually injured states by continuous aggression have been so injured in their affections that they do not dare trust love. Afraid to show kindness, they also resist affection as a dangerous prelude to more injury. They may get a morbid satisfaction out of injuring others, or, in lieu of that, may find it safer to inflict harm upon themselves. Because love presents a hazard to them, their pattern is to injure before they get injured. Competition drains off much of this emotional state in our culture, but when persons are not able to work it off satisfactorily in such ways they turn against the more helpless; they are cruel toward animals or children or those in their employ.

Sometimes hard work uses up the aggressive impulse, and competitive sports give it an acceptable outlet. If people can be led to understand the source of their feelings, they may be able to resolve them. Often, however, they use even the offices of religion to pursue their emotional needs. Understanding their needs can make it possible to understand their aggressive acts and attitudes. Still, until the inner balance of their lives is changed by a redemptive love that they can accept, there is little chance of changing their natures by gentle persuasion, since any kindness is interpreted as weakness and any weakness is but an invitation to express their hatred safely.

Often the spiritually injured are deeply confused. They do not understand their feelings or what happens to them as the result of them. Their energies are used up by continuous inner civil wars that produce no good fruits while at the same time depleting their resources for living. They often complain of fatigue, and about most other circumstances of life as well. They appear drawn and haggard, as if they did more than their share of the world's work, when actually they have insufficient energy for their work. They often become ill with diseases that bring life to a standstill. They project into religious activity their states of confusion. Their problem is one of finding the self that should be in command so that they can organize and marshall the energy of life toward constructive goals. Often these people are responsive to the counseling process, for they want to find a way out of their dilemma and are willing to use their energy toward such goals as may emerge from new insight. But many times the confusion they express about religious matters is but a latch-string hung out as an invitation for help with their real problems.

The people who show their spiritual injuries through states of anxiety are revealing that the value structures of their lives are seriously threatened. They are apprehensive lest life fall apart, and they do not know where to turn to make things secure. Although they have not the self-assurance to understand the real cause-effect relationships of their fears, they often respond to a process that helps them to face realities, and are willing to do the immediate constructive acts needed to clarify the total picture of their living. When they find that some problems can be handled effectively, they move toward more clearly defined goals. Since these people are usually tense and apprehensive, just the mood and atmosphere of relaxation can be helpful to them: they are reassured when their anxiety is not contagious. The disciplines of small group spiritual development can often be useful for the anxious. In the atmosphere of meditation and quietness, they feel a quietness settling down over them. The use of specific techniques of relaxation employed by physicians resolves the physical tension and sets in motion a calming effect of emotions and attitudes of mind.

The conditions under which many people live today tend to produce emotional states that are spiritually injuring. The pastor can help to make the total life of the church free from pressures and calming to the lives of those who share it. This can be done, first of all, by his own attitude. If he gives the impression of the harried man beset by problems rather than uplifted by solutions, he can project that harassment into the life of the parish. If, on the other hand, he calmly approaches the tasks and problems of parish life as if he were part of the solution rather than part of the problem, he can give assurance and serenity to those who are continually watching to see if his spiritual resources are showing.

His special concern for those who come to him in their anguish enables him to use his unique competence to guide the distressed through their crises in life and toward a more mature and competent handling of their own existence. This ministry to the spiritually injured is not easy, and it can well tax the skills and emotional resources of the pastor, but it is not without its rewards.

11

PASTORAL CARE THROUGH
GROUPS

WHEREVER the life of the church has been vigorous and productive, the power of the small group has been actively used to stimulate creative action. Jesus entrusted the fate of his movement to a small group of men whom he had carefully trained. The monastic tradition was

159

started as a small group movement of men who withdrew from the community to purify their own inner life in shared spiritual experience. John Wesley organized his reform movement within the Church of England by using small groups, prayer bands for exploration and personal sharing, classes for study and personal enrichment. The Quaker movement and the Oxford group movement have both found their strength in special processes that work within the dynamic nature of the small but stimulating relationship of group experience.

Psychologists and psychotherapists have rediscovered the value of the small group for counseling and therapeutic procedures. Some of this was discovered quite by accident, such as the improvement shown by outpatients in a TB clinic when they were given instructions in how to understand their symptoms. With understanding came improvement, and with the improvement came an assurance shared within the group as all moved toward new health by the process. During the war group therapy began as an economy measure. Since the few psychotherapists could not treat in private sessions the many pilots suffering from flight fatigue, they began to see them in small groups and found that there was something in the very life of the group that hastened progress toward health. In a hospital for mental cases it was observed that patients in a ward made better progress than the wealthier patients who were able to afford private rooms. The chance to share experience with others in a small group is therapeutically significant. Thus a whole new interest in the powers of the small group has developed in recent years, and qualified experts affirm the fact that the small group can add important values to life and movement to the therapeutic process.

Traditionally, the life of the parish is filled with small group activities. Committees, social affairs, study groups, youth groups, and classes all share the problems and privileges of small group dynamics The wise understanding of what goes on in these aggregations of human beings can make it possible for such activities to bear rich fruit in personality growth. But does the average pastor meet with a committee as if it were an end in itself, or as if it might become a means to the larger goals of personality development? Is the church concerned only with what a group or organization accomplishes, or does it use the small group as a resource to help people relate to each other, express their feelings, clarify their vision, and grow into fuller life?

Such questions open up possibilities of renewing the inner life of the church by the wise use of resources that have been traditionally an important part of its life. If we are to use small groups wisely, though, it is important to know some of the dynamic forces that are at work among people in this context—forces different in a group from those operative in individual counseling. In the individual relationship the counselor is accepting and uncritical, in order to establish rapport, so that the newly gained insights of the counseling relationship may lead to new feelings for others. In the group situation the establishing of a group goal immediately enlists both the thoughts and the feelings toward specific ends.

In individual counseling the counselee works out his problems of relationship with a counselor who is, for him, an emotional focus such as a father figure. In the group relationship the setting involves many personalities and the process of relating to them is apt to follow the more normal and dynamic pattern of the family emotional structure.

In his relationship to the counselee, the counselor may adopt a permissive attitude, not only to establish rapport but also to demonstrate the faith in human relationships so essential to growth in insight. In the group pattern the rapport with the leader is not as important as the dynamics of the group itself, for the rejection of the leader by the group may be a way of resolving an emotional pattern within the group. The pastor has to be aware of this when his leadership is rejected by a committee that chooses a course of independent action. It may be an essential growth experience within the group. Often this will be noted with an adolescent group whose quest for independence may encourage rebellion against any authority that represents a parent figure.

The dynamics of the individual counseling relationship may be more intense and less varied. Resistance and resentment may be sharply defined and require the understanding of a skilled counselor. Within the group the emotional responses are apt to be more varied but less intense because the number of personality response patterns is multipied.

All of these factors have to be considered as dynamics at work in meeting the needs of the individual who becomes part of a group. But while the dynamics in a group may operate without specific relationship to the leader, his influence is considerable. His ability to sense and respond to the needs of the group is important to the development of group attitudes and feelings.

The pastor's role in group leadership is important not only as it reflects his understanding of groups, but also as it indicates his emotional needs as reflected in his own behavior. The tyrant sets goals and uses any power at his disposal to accomplish his purposes. He is not open to suggestion, nor is he responsive to the group. Because of certain emotional needs the group may accept this leadership, but the group is not free and it does not usually experience growth. Some pastors assume a patriarchal-sovereign type of leadership role. Their wishes are dominant; a benevolent and paternal attitude is used only to exert influence. People who disagree are made to feel disloyal, and the leader makes his feelings the primary guide for the group, rather than being responsive to theirs. Such a group is thwarted from expressing its feelings because it is made to feel guilty by doing so. Such a group cannot be democratic in action, but when emotional needs within the group warrant it, such leadership is accepted.

Sometimes a skilled leader will use a group. He will identify with the group, largely to manipulate it. He will invite cooperation in reaching goals that he sets himself. While his attitude is not rigid, he uses his position as leader to move the group in a direction he sets.

This is in contrast to the democratic type of leadership which would have the group become aware of its own needs and use the resources of the group to fulfill them. This democratic leadership skillfully throws back into the group the matter of decision. The leader keeps his own feelings and desires subservient to the group's needs. He feels that the group process is both an end and a means—what the group does is not so important as how well it learns to do it by and for itself.

Just as leadership varies, so do groups vary. Some are temporary but highly significant. Others are more permanent and the influences are more gradual and subtle. A child may attend church school for years without developing any significant change in his ideas, but a week at a summer conference may have great impact mentally and emotionally.

The group involves both a relationship and a process. It is built on the dynamics of inter-relatedness within a group, subject to skilled guidance by a leader who understands the powerful influences at work and the needs of the group as it grows toward mutually acceptable goals. Essentially the group is something more than the sum total of its members. Things can happen in a group which none of its members could do alone. When these forces are negative and destructive, we have riots and lynchings. When they are creative and positive, we have high points of courage and achievement.

Jesus recognized the need for group relationship. He spoke of himself as a shepherd. He tried to help people overcome their sense of separation from their rightful groupings. As with the woman at the well in Samaria, as with the lost sheep and the lost son and other lost individuals, he sought to restore a creative working relationship with the group.

The skilled observer of group forces is sensitive to what

happens to people within a group. He knows that people may be cruelly injured by a group as well as helped by it. It is the pastor's task to understand the forces at work so that they may be used more helpfully and so that their injurious effect may be reduced.

Church-related group life has a clear advantage, for its purposes do not have to depend on raw competition or on aggressive action. Dr. Martin Grotjahn, a psychiatrist, emphasizes this when he writes, "It is much easier to activate group emotions of hostile opposition and destruction than of tolerance and cooperation. A group feels strength in hate and fight. The group feels broken up into weak individuals when love and cooperation is asked. Only the religious group is firm in faith and belief. It is united, and, therefore, does not need hatred as a unifying factor." If this is true, and my experience confirms it, the religious group has a strategic position, for it is consciously and unconsciously related to the release of creative emotions. Life needs love and acceptance to sustain it. A competitive culture and a conflicting international order leave little room for healthy emotions. The singular contribution of the church and its group life is made more explicit by contrast. The religious group can move toward mature and helpful action, rather than stimulating a reversion to more primitive and injurious expressions of emotion. Where self-interest is paramount, the more primitive emotions are stimulated. Where interest in the needs of others is inspired, the action of the group can become self-sacrificing and heroic.

The individual tends to take on the emotional color of the group. If the group is frightened, he shares the fear. In a London bomb shelter, where no damage was done and no physical cause of death existed, more than two hundred persons died in one night through a shattering fear that gripped the group. On life rafts in the Pacific men often lived for weeks with little food or water because of the inspired leadership of one courageous man who supplied the emotional tone for the group.

Conscious and subconscious factors tend to create dependence on the group. A primitive desire for relatedness often causes people to modify their own standards in order to be accepted by the group. The fear of separation may be greater than conviction. The sense of insecurity apart from the group may invite compromise and even change of personality structure. This may be either negative or positive depending on the group.

The basic emotional needs of the individual are always satisfied in relation to certain group formations. Emotional security comes through the family, acculturation through the school group, vocation through the employment group and meaning for life through the religious group. When the individual functions normally within his group, it meets his needs and he contributes to group goals. But when an individual is injured by the group relationship to the extent that he withdraws, it is reasonable to believe that he will suffer severely unless the old relationship can be reestablished or a new and satisfactory substitute found.

Within the group life of the church, whether it be committees whose purposes seems prescribed, or in those groups where the needs of the members is the main focal point of action, we have people in action. Their behavior is always meaningful to the skilled observer, and the freedom with which they are able to function may well be a clue as to how useful the group is to them in working through those personal growth problems that involve everyone. For instance, a man who uses committee life for aggressive action by vigorously opposing the opinions of others may be meeting a need for a safe outlet for his angry feelings. A widow in a spiritual life study group may use the framework of the group not only to work through her grief but also as a repository for those frustated emotions that can no longer be directed toward her husband, yet do need a safe and reasonable place for their reinvestment.

The forms of behavior within a group are apt to be less guarded and more direct than those which would be shown toward an individual counselor. The actions may be quick, energetic, and decisive. The relationships tend to be clear and uncomplicated, and therefore especially revealing of what is going on within the person. A person may use the group as a place for bragging, or for sympathy, or for acceptance. In each instance he is saying that he seeks within the group status, emotional support, or love. When the group process moves freely, its individual members tend to pass open and critical judgments upon each other. This candor is common in group practice, and helps members of the group to face themselves as they might not otherwise do. This stimulates growth in self-understanding, and makes some of the often used defenses less effective.

Some of the things that happen in groups do not appear to happen in the separate life of the individual. The New Testament implies that the Holy Spirit comes more easily in an atmosphere stimulated by group action. Jerome Frank points out that primitive healing often involved an obligation within the group to do something for someone else. This directs attention away from the self and gives a new focal interest. Often the breakdown of life comes when a person feels he is no longer needed. In the employment group this is made explicit through retirement; in the family group through the departure from home of the young. In the military group it is made dramatic by replacement and reassignment. The need for new group alignments to keep life interesting continually shows itself as old group relationships break down. The church may serve a useful purpose through the numerous and varied forms of its group life.

In an apartment house community, a man who had always enjoyed working around his own home found self-expression, a need for his services, and a creative fellowship by participating in a work group that spent one evening a week doing repairs and other chores around the church property. A group of retired men spent one afternoon a week together in recreation. A group of parents of adolescents found new understanding of each other and their children in shared experience and new information. A group of elderly women worked together for the hospital and felt useful as they enjoyed each other's company.

Vernon L., an only child, lived with his doting, widowed mother until her death. After she died, when Vernon was in his thirties, he married a woman who carried on the mothering process. Vernon was "touchy," sensitive to any slight, and continually complaining about imagined abuses. The first Sunday he attended church in a new community no one made a fuss over him, and he expressed adverse opinions about the church. In time he was nevertheless nominated for a committee assignment. At meetings he acted as if he were doing the committee a favor by serving on it. But his fellow-members were mature and perceptive. They considered his suggestions carefully and referred some back to him for action. Without any implied judgment, they created the feeling that words were to be supported by actions. Before long he had assumed a less vocal role, yet was beginning to find satisfaction in working out ideas with other members of the committee. In a community where he might not have been accepted he began to find friendship. In order to maintain that friendship he gradually began to conform to the standards of behavior and the general attitude of those who were his friends. After three years he was given a position of leadership which carried the status he desired; and indeed, he had earned the right to lead by his changed attitude toward group activity.

The religious group has a special advantage, for it organizes life about spiritual goals that do not wear out but become more important as life moves on. Something healthy, innate in group life, continues to work in the lives of the committees and boards, work sessions and study groups that are a part of nearly all church life. Jerome Frank says that "clinical experience clearly suggests that group patients tend to reinforce each other's healthy reactions and correct each other's neurotic ones." If people can be kept together within a program of varied group activities, this inner corrective will be continually at work.

Often in parish work we think of groups as ends in themselves, with clearly defined purposes. A finance committee is, however, not limited to raising and spending money, for it is made up of people with feelings and needs who do useful things with and to each other as they work together. The property committee is more than a group of people whose sole purpose is keeping property in order. These committees are always a means to an end at the same time that they serve specific ends. The group process always reminds us of the fact that the means is part of the end; a group life that helps people work out deep emotional needs is not only meeting certain group goals, but is also satisfying the expressed and unexpressed needs of the individual members.

The pastor who explores the current research in group dynamics, group therapy, and the improvement of group procedures will improve his understanding of the group life of his parish. He will find a ready-made resource to help people understand themselves and those with whom they must live. He will find a deeper dimension in those varied activities that make up the group life of the church, and will see meanings in group processes that had escaped him before.

The pastor who develops his skills in using group processes will find that these become an ally in his work with individuals. And what is more, he will gain through his own involvement in the group life of the church a warmth and freedom his own life needs. The deeper meanings of group life and resources for growth through group processes present an inviting aspect for development of church programs. The pastor who discerns these deeper meanings has an already established framework through which his insights can be expressed and find verification.

12

PASTORAL CARE
THROUGH INSTITUTIONS

*T*HE CHAPLAINCY PROGRAMS that many institutions have set up in recent years afford us a rare chance to take a more discerning look at the pastor's task in institutions. These chaplains, with their special training and sensitivities, have made us so aware of the opportunities afforded in hospitals, homes, prisons and among other groups of segregated persons, that the parish minister should never again take lightly or perform in perfunctory fashion the tasks that institutions present.

Our concern in this chapter is primarily with those special types of care that are required by the ill in body, mind and spirit in the hospital setting; the care of the aged in the homes for the aged; and the problems that meet the pastor who visits imprisoned members. Although the military chaplaincy is a vital and rewarding phase of the ministry, this function is outside the scope of this chapter.

The family is an institution within the church, of course, and it has its special problems and privileges. And the university and other schools of higher learning are often institutions of the church. But the pastor's tasks with the family and with the student members of the parish have received adequate treatment elsewhere, and so we will place them, too, outside the scope of this chapter.

The institutional tasks of the pastor are determined usually by two factors—first, the number and location of the institutions within his community. And second, the location of his institutionalized parishoners. He usually has at least a semi-official relationship to the institution, is known and recognized by members of the staff, and is accepted in his role as pastor. With the institutionalized parishioners, however, he may be only an occasional visitor in surroundings that are unfamiliar and sometimes forbidding. In either instance, his basic task is the same—to reach an individual, in a setting that is apt to limit or deny his feeling of individual worth, with a message of acceptance and understanding and a concern for mediating God's healing, redeeming love.

The way people develop is continually being modified by circumstances, and the pastor may well be one of the circumstances.

Let us start with the most difficult of institutional ministries, that of the prisoners in a correctional institution. Here is a captive audience if there ever was one.

The pastor has a privileged relationship in visiting in county, state and federal correctional institutions. He is granted opportunities that are denied to others. He can come and go with considerable freedom, and because of his priestly role he has the chance for private communications not usually allowed. In nearby institutions he may call in person, yet communication by mail to persons a long distance from the parish should not be discounted.

Charles S., in his early twenties, had been closely related to the church until employment threw him into contact with a different type of person. He became involved in grand larceny and was imprisoned for three years. The prison was several hundred miles away and the pastor made no personal visits. Through letters, however, he was able to maintain relations and prepare a way for return to the world outside.

The initial communication was merely an expression of concern that Charles was obliged to spend part of his life in this way, but it also indicated that even such circumstances could be turned to a good end with effort. Shortly thereafter, in a letter to his parents, Charles expressed confusion about the meaning of life. He said he would like the pastor to send him certain material to read. No direct letters were received by the pastor (because prison requirements limited letters to one each week, and these went to the parents). But through the parents regular communication was maintained by and with the pastor. The pastor's letters were directed to the comments in letters to the parents, yet even under such difficult limits the communication was fruitful.

When emotional conditions are acute, the most limited types of contact may be far more fruitful than is usually realized. Charles read and reread every letter. He read and reread each pamphlet and book. In fact, within prison walls he took a graduate course in the meaning of life and the nature of religion. As the time for his release approached, efforts were directed toward finding creative employment that would make it possible for him to be free of the influences that had been damaging in the past.

Now the most difficult part of the experience is past and Charles is studying in a school of commercial art in a nearby city in preparation for employment that is already promised. Contact was maintained under difficult conditions, but it seems that the effort was productive because the correspondent was receptive. This, of course, is not always the case.

The person classified by society as a criminal is often sociopathic, one who works out his maladjustments through a direct assault on society rather than internalizing them in neurotic symptoms. With such people there seems to be no basis for contact; the ability to feel warm human relations has been damaged so badly that other people are "allowed" to exist only to be manipulated for personal gain. The hardened criminal is separated emotionally from the channels of normal affective life. His mood is suspicious of all who do not share his way of life. Although the pastor usually observes little fruitful change in the life of the sociopath, it is doubtful that any person is completely beyond reach. There are those who are easily approached and those whose emotional scars are so deep that they protect themselves more vigorously from what they fear will be injuring human contacts. But in normal pastoral work, little is achieved with occasional contacts with a sociopathic personality.

More is accomplished with the person whose brush with the law came about through accidental circumstances rather than emotional predisposition. These are people involved in motor vehicle crimes, and those who commit crimes during temporary emotional states due to stress, or to solve problems so overwhelming that these people have temporarily lost their focus on life. Such people feel true guilt, remorse, and separation from the community. They are frightened by what has happened, confused by the variety of reactions of others toward them in their plight, and apprehensive about the future. Often they are deeply depressed, though they may use various methods to keep from showing it.

People who suffer from these complex emotions do not present a simple case for pastoral counseling. But guilt may, quite contrary to general psychiatric thought, be one of the healthiest of human emotions. Just as grief is an indication of the value that is placed upon life, so guilt is the barometer that gauges the intensity of feeling for social order. With feelings of true guilt, the energy of life can be employed to shape a wiser future.

175

Leslie L. is a case to illustrate this point. His pastor visited him in the county jail, to which Leslie had been sentenced to a year less one day. A prominent member of the community, he had been a leader in local industry and active in athletic and social circles. He had always been a sober and dependable person until financial stress led him to embezzle funds from his company. Leslie confessed his crime when auditors discovered the discrepancy in the books. While he admitted his guilt technically, he did not want to accept it emotionally. When his pastor first visited him Leslie tried to blame others, and in a variety of ways showed that he was not ready to accept the true meaning of his guilt. He claimed that after "years of service to the company" they had a moral obligation to him greater than the amount of money involved. He sought to avoid the full meaning of his behavior by thinking of himself as "framed." When the pastor accepted his angry feelings but refused to support them, Leslie L. seemed affronted. During subsequent visits he said less and less about other people and began to talk more about himself and flaws in his character that he had been aware of but had failed to correct. He said, "I knew it wasn't right but I was weak." He examined the causes of his weakness. When he was able to look squarely at his guilt he was in a position to examine his behavior, assess the results of it, and make plans for the future with a clearer concept of the bounds that one must impose upon himself in order to function in society.

When he came out of jail he had another job awaiting him, and he has slowly worked his way back into the life of the community. A difficult circumstance that might have left him in bitterness and resentment was worked through with a pastor willing to give him time in difficult surroundings. Leslie L. has emerged with courage to face the community and rebuild his life among those who know the worst about him, but who also are willing to expect something better. This resource could not be separated from the insights that were developed through a counseling process which recognized the constructive nature of guilt and the need to channel its emotional energies toward wiser future action.

The military guard house, or the local jail where a youth may be spending his first night away from home, or the penitentiary where society exacts its larger punishment—all create an environment where strong emotions are at work. Wise management of these emotional crises has great significance for the ongoing process of life. No pastor can ignore the opportunity afforded him to work within the walls of a correctional institution.

Quite in contrast is the ministry performed for residents of nursing homes, convalescent homes, and homes for retired and elderly people. The previous chapter concerned itself with the psychological factors involved in the aging process, and with suggestions as to how to deal with them. Here we would merely emphasize that people living within such institutional environments afford an opportunity for a special ministry that may have great meaning for them.

The chief preoccupation of the aged is with their own death. This thought is either actively expressed or forced out of consciousness in conversation. Yet the chief existential questions concerning life have a right to be answered. The days of terminal illness and the months of wasting away may appear to be accompanied by a state of lessened interest and withdrawal from feeling and experiences. But often this is in appearance only. The mind shut off from sensory experience may still race with thoughts and ideas. When the aged person craves communication most, everyone else may seem so busy that he finally gives up. In deep inner despair, he feels no one cares what he thinks or how he feels. The pastor who shares such moments may well help prepare a soul for the coming of death.

A staff psychiatrist in a large city hospital, whose chief function is work with patients in terminal illness, reports fruitful and active communication with many of his patients who yearn for a chance to explore verbally the edges of the mystery that will soon engulf them. The word of faith, the assurance of the existence of the soul that is not measured by space and time, may well be the most valued contribution that a pastor can make to the lives of his aged parishioners. It is no hardship to talk about death. It is one of the rich privileges of the pastoral ministry openly and honestly to explore the boundaries of human existence with those who have lived the long years and whose days are now nearly over.

Without doubt the institutional ministry claiming most of the pastor's time and attention is his work in the hospital. Types of hospital vary. In a small city, one serves all comers; in a large city there are specialized institutions for every type of ailment and condition—hospitals for acute and chronic ailments, for so-called incurable diseases, and for disturbances of mind and emotion. During several years as a chaplain in general and specialized hospitals, the author found the main characteristic of pastoral care to be a struggle toward right relationships, with the patient making his important contributions and the pastor offering a cluster of roles and ministries from which the patient might select according to his needs.

Part of this ministry is in a specialized type of counseling, aware of special physical conditions, of the intensity of emotions and of the opportunity that comes with such critical life situations. Such was the case with Mrs. Rummell. Her daughter called the pastor and said that her mother was acutely ill at the local hospital, that her strength was waning fast, and that the physicians held out little hope for her survival.

The pastor went immediately to the hospital, found the patient alone in her room, and made an initial noncommital remark. The patient expressed a strong death wish, and attributed her anguished state of spirit to the fact that her daughter had gone against her wishes in marrying a "foreigner." The patient expressed resentment against her son-in-law, his name, his family, his national origin. Then she burst into tears and said, "Oh, why do I feel this way about him?" This led to more purgation; as if she were squeezing the core out of a boil, she exuded poisoned emotions.

We talked briefly about the young man as a person, and moved into a mood of prayer. When it was over she said, "I don't know why I feel better, but I do." The next day she was improved and a week or so later was returned home in good health. The family tried to claim that a miracle had happened, but the brief interview with its confession, expurgation and prayer for forgiveness was not magical. It was simply an exercise in restoring right relationships, and it undoubtedly had an effect upon the body chemistry and the internal mechanisms that control health.

Recent studies of psychotherapeutic methods place a renewed emphasis on the value of those procedures that engage the total being, rather than on just the thought processes. This is obviously important in working in an institution for the mentally and emotionally ill. No discernible difference can be found between one school of treatment and another; this makes it difficult to champion any one type of treatment above another. It does make it possible, however, to give equal value to those methods of treatment that employ religious values and ritualized techniques to reach the total person.

Certain ritualized acts satisfy deep emotional needs, and in so doing may serve important therapeutic purposes. The feeling that some religious acts may be injurious to the mentally or emotionally ill person does not seem valid in the light of recent studies. Even the responses that superficially appear to be injurious may, in the long run, serve healthful purposes. The administering of sacraments, tending as it does to relate a person to a tradition of healthful participation, is important. And the implication of forgiveness and renewal of life may reach more deeply to the needs of the personality than can any words uttered.

Nor should the ministry of things be overlooked. In some instances withdrawn patients who had shown no interest in their surroundings, and had failed to participate in any but the most basic biological functions, responded when a birthday cake was presented to them. Something that had long been suppressed came to life with the symbolic gift and the healthful memories clustered about it. Actually we know so little about the processes that produce and relieve mental illness that it is unwise to overlook any associative act that could trigger a healthful response.

In some hospital settings the preaching ministry is included. Through a system of loud speakers, chapel services are broadcast in wards and private rooms. While this may enlarge the audience, it also increases the responsibility of the preacher to keep in mind the seriously ill and disturbed patient as well as those who are ambulatory.

One objection heard often about the ministry in hospitals is that it tends to disregard the rules of the hospital and the best interests of the patients. Some efforts at religious healing within the hospitals have not only been disdainful of medical practice but have been discourteous to those granting the privilege of the special service. The hospital is clearly the domain of the physician. While medicine in general recognizes the contribution that religious practice can make to wholeness of being, it does not welcome acts or attitudes that disregard the traditions and disciplines of the medical profession.

The pastor enters the hospital ward as a person concerned about the thoughts and feelings of the patient. In an atmosphere of baffling and confusing phrases and routines, the patient may cling to a familiar voice or face as a source of security. The pastor never needs to apologize for the special ministry he performs, for although it may be different from that of the physician, it has its own significance and value.

The pastoral ministry in the institution has too often been treated lightly. The times when emotions are heightened are times when important life changes may take place. A few minutes shared with a person in a time of crisis can be far more significant than many hours spent in trivial social affairs. The chance to relate to people when their feelings are close to the surface may be the most rewarding part of the pastoral ministry.

In recent years institutional chaplains have written excellent books defining the methods and opportunities of these specialized ministries. These books warrant careful study, for they open doors to a more fruitful use of the circumstances offered by hospitals, homes and correctional institutions. These people are never beyond the parish, if the parish is understood as people who need to commune and communicate. Often the pastor with his privileged status becomes the key figure in the life of the institutionalized parishioner.

13

PASTORAL CARE THROUGH PARISH CALLING

*T*HE Rev. Mr. T. J. was making a regular parish call. He approached the front door, as he had so many hundreds of times during his ministry. As he put his finger on the doorbell, he had no way of knowing that a gas pipe leak in the kitchen had produced just the right amount of gas to create an explosive mixture with the oxygen in the kitchen. Nor did he know that the buzzer connected with the front door button would produce a spark sufficient to set off the explosive mixture. Never had he had so immediate a response to a pastoral call! When he pushed the front doorbell, the back end of the dwelling blew out. It is not unreasonable to think that the Rev. Mr. T. J. now has some unusual feelings when he makes his regular rounds of pastoral calls.

Most pastors do. These feelings are the result of years of calling on all types of people under all kinds of conditions. George Buttrick tells of calling again and again at an apartment in his neighborhood, only to be informed by the butler that no one was at home. But when a crisis developed in that family he was called, so even the calls he made when no one would admit to being at home were not wasted.

A woman who answered the door in what she considered inappropriate attire, thinking she had only to make a payment to the insurance man, was chagrined when she recognized her pastor standing there. She never came to church again, because she said she could not get over her embarrassment. It would have been better had the pastor not stopped there that day.

Robert McCracken tells of visiting a cantankerous old lady who was very critical of him and everything he did. Although no answer came to his repeated knocks, he thought he heard a rustling on the other side of the door. On a sudden impulse—never repeated—he looked through the keyhole and saw the blue eyes of his parishioner. With quick wit he said into the keyhole, "Mrs. McPherson, I am glad that we at last see eye to eye on something."

Any pastor who has done much calling could describe countless experiences, both amusing and revealing, about parish calling. But one must look beneath the anecdotes to consider whether calling is good or bad, wise or foolish, wasteful or productive.

Perhaps no part of the work of the modern minister is more debated than the practice of pastoral calling. Some men who have a gift for preaching and administration feel that calling is a waste of time. They say, "Why should I spend my time in small talk and parish gossip, or in listening to the woes of the hypochondriac, when there are so many other things that need to be done?"

The man who is carefully trained in counseling and pastoral care may well feel that his special training is wasted in the traditional pattern of parish calling. He may say, "I have developed special skills to help my people. Why should I engage in time-consuming tasks that produce little or no fruit, when those who appreciate my skill and would really use it are clamoring for attention?"

Even the man who has devoted himself diligently to the tasks of parish calling is aware of its problems; many people, quite obviously, do not want to see a minister. Under such circumstances the call seems not only to be useless but to have negative results. The organization of the parish now places demands upon the pastor which did not exist in church work a generation or two ago. The pastor finds less and less time for the traditional pattern of calling. What, then, is to be done with this aspect of pastoral work?

We must first consider the traditional pattern of pastoral calling. The pastor was expected to call from house to house in the parish, sometimes on a geographical basis where several members in a neighborhood would be called on in an afternoon. By going up one side of the street and coming down the other, the pastor not only saw a number of his flock, he also created a mild form of consternation as members looking out of their windows wondered if they would be next. Should they make a cake, dare they go to the store, or what dress should they wear? The call tended to be social in nature and its religious activity probably consisted of a scripture reading and prayer, perfunctory at best. Because everything was at rather a routine or social level, there was little actual pastoral counseling as we now know it.

If the visits were scheduled on an alphabetical basis, which became practical with the advent of the automobile, some of the less desirable factors of the geographical call were eliminated, yet still the routine and social nature of the relationship tended to persist.

This type of call had special values. It brought the pastor into active, though informal, contact with the family in a way that showed his interest and concern and gave status to the person who occupied the pew. In rural areas such a visit was important for the more significant social function of the church. Also, one probably could not count the number of youth directed toward the ministry by a pastor who asked, "And, young man, have you thought about what *you* are going to be when you grow up?"

The fragmentation of the family, however, has changed all that. A daytime house call is seldom a family call, for rarely is there anyone at home except perhaps a housewife who is embarrassed because she does not feel properly dressed to receive a call from her pastor.

In most instances even the sick call fails to serve the purpose it once did. There was a time when a sick call was a useful family call, when all members of the family gathered around the sick bed, and all of their needs could be approached at one time. Now most illness is treated in a hospital, and seldom is there a chance to meet with the family as a unit.

Thus, the new approach to pastoral calling is not dictated primarily by the pastor himself, but rather is an outgrowth of a variety of gradually developed factors. The nature of the demands that the community makes on the pastor tend to shape and direct both his training and his practice.

Probably no pastor escapes the comparison that older members of the parish make between his practice of pastoral calling and that of a predecessor who lived and served two generations ago. Such comparisons, compounded of nostalgia, failing memory, and resentment tend to discredit the modern practice. But consider this simple comparison of statistics: Brother D. served a parish when there were a hundred families in its membership. He was credited with making a call on each family three or four times a year. His total would probably have been about 350 calls, with no pastoral counseling, quite limited organizational work and little, if any, community or social service work. His calls were leisurely, friendly, and long-remembered because of his vibrant personality and his ability as a raconteur. His calls were geared to the tempo of his day, and in that time he did his work wisely and well.

In contrast, his contemporary successor in the same parish

187

must meet the needs of more than a thousand members. This rapidly changing suburban district is served by a number of city hospitals. In the course of a year his members are hospitalized in as many as sixteen different institutions located from four to thirty-five miles away. Numerous organizational meetings, the inevitable building programs, and a variety of community demands, added to his thousand pastoral calls and his five hundred hours of pastoral counseling, keep him engaged day and night. With the schedule our modern pastor keeps, he could have made a home call once a month in that parish as it was two generations ago. But few there are who seem to recognize the difference in parishes and in ministerial responsibility. If there is any one point where the pastor is subject to criticism, it is at the point of pastoral calling. Though he may be doing more than has ever been done before in the parish, the nature of the demands in the parish obscure, confuse, and distort what is done. Even the official members of the parish have little understanding of the nature of a day's work on the part of their pastor.

This was borne out when the official board in a local parish was asked to advise the pastor on the best use of his time. Different individuals were asked to note the amount of time they felt would be reasonable, if not ideal, for specific phases of the minister's work. The purpose was to be practical and useful, rather than idealistic. The results jarred the board as well as the pastor, for in their effort to be helpful, they outlined a work week that totaled 155 hours.

In evaluating pastoral calling, we must move beyond the unrealistic view of the minister's work that even the well-informed parishioner seems to possess. So that he does not violate his own integrity of function, the pastor must face the changing concept of pastoral care in the total work of the ministry as he also tries to relate his own specialized training to the needs of his people.

In some ways this resembles a tight rope performance. For the parish is not a static situation. People are increasingly urged to talk with their pastor about personal problems. This leads to an active demand by a small segment of the parish for specialized help. While this may be good, in the sense that those conscious of their need may be most readily helped, it also means that direct pressure by certain types of persons is a fact to contend with. The demands of the person ringing the pastor's doorbell may interfere with that other part of the pastoral ministry that involves his ringing of doorbells.

Without a clear allotment of time and a careful definition of function, some of the special privileges involved in the pastoral call may be overlooked. Of all those who work with people, the pastor has a special privilege in ready access to the homes of his people. This is important in seeking out the timid whose needs may be considerable, in gaining a breadth of perspective relating to the family constellation, and in assessing individual and group needs as they are reflected in a natural habitat.

Anyone skilled in dealing with personality needs is well aware that often those whose needs are most acute are least aware of it. The excessively suspicious, aggressive, or disoriented may deny any subjective element in their mental or emotional state. With an ever increasing disruptive effect, they tend to project their subjective state into the environment around them. The opportunity for a skilled observer to get into the situation is rather remote just when it might be most productive. The pastor's situation is unique in that he does not have to wait for referral. He can serve both as an agency for treatment and an instrument for referral, if it seems wise.

In order to function well in this specialized role, it is important to discard the old methods of routine calling, and set up a set of values in accord with specialized training and evaluation of the pastoral function. This calls for a hierarchy of calling, with some types of calls taking precedence over others.

Those calls that deal with emotional or spiritual emergencies, such as illness, death, acute personal or family problems, and crises in individual or group life must rate high on the list of calls. Often these open opportunities for pastoral care that are rare privileges. The pastor at the scene of a fire in the home of one of his parishioners who invited the burned-out family to stay at the parsonage until they got reorganized, set the scene for dealing with a case of acute anxiety that probably could not have been dealt with as satisfactorily in a more formal relationship. When a careless inebriate set a fire that caused the death of a young child, the haven of the parsonage made it possible to work through an aggressive impulse of murderous proportions before it could bring double tragedy upon a distressed family.

It certainly is not pastoral counseling in the generally accepted framework, but it is a ministry to people that gets to them when their need is greatest. This may characterize the parish ministry that is willing to go to people at those moments of need that can precipitate emotional crises.

The community grants the pastor a special status in ministering to the bereaved. He should be immediately at the scene of parishioner's need and remain close by during the days of acute stress. This gives him a chance to use his special knowledge to implement the expression of normal emotions, to prevent the building of a structure of illusion that denies reality, and also to help direct activity toward that new orientation of thought and feeling that must accompany any adjustment to the death of an important person in life. Close association in times of stress builds bridges of understanding. These can serve later to institute those more normal processes of pastoral counseling that may be needed to handle problems of delayed grief reactions.

Perhaps no area of pastoral calling has been treated with as much skill and fullness as the care of the sick. Little need be added here, except that the extra time available and the special needs that exist at times of illness often open doors to a pastoral relationship that is fruitful in producing spiritual insight.

A second group of calls, farther down the list of priorities, are those to the aged, the newcomers, the newly married, the parents of the newly born, and those organizational calls that are inevitably a part of church life. As an initial contact these calls build a basis for confidence and human interest that can mature into effective pastoral counseling. When a board member showed unusual aggressiveness, the pastor followed it up with a concern for the inner distress that caused the aggression. This led into a discussion that produced insight and genuine movement in the personality of the afflicted member, and it did the board no damage in the process.

A third type of call is purely social. Yet skillfully used, even here is real opportunity for pastoral care. There is good biblical precedent for going fishing with the boys. A camping trip with scouts, a ride in the country with aged members, a house-hunting expedition with new prospects in the community, may not fulfill the requirements of formal pastoral work, but they can pay real dividends in the human relationships that are vital to effective parish work.

With all of this in mind, it is important to remember that the pastor's function differs from that of any other of the skilled professional workers with people. His function gives him a broader approach to people and they know it. For that reason it is practically impossible for a pastor to carry on a non-directive approach to his people. He may try to fulfill all of the book requirements for such a counseling procedure. But the fact that he is a minister, who preaches on Sunday and can call in the home during the week, gives to his counseling a predisposing factor not present in the insulated atmosphere of the psychologist or the psychiatrist. Even the counseling room of the pastor, no matter how closely it may resemble the room of a psychologist, is a different place because the pastor is a different person. He may not know it and may not encourage any such ideas. But the idea is planted early in life and nourished through the years; even the closed door of a counseling room does not separate the counselee from all of his feelings about what ministers are and do.

In many respects this is a disadvantage, for the pastor with special skills has to contend with prejudicial attitudes on the part of many of his parishioners. But on the other hand, this attitude can be an important ally in reaching feelings not so easily accessible to the secular counselor.

Since many disturbances in the souls of people are close to religious consciousness, they respond more readily to an approach that starts with an awareness of their spiritual nature. While this is not the atmosphere of piety and judgment, it is the mood of concern, awareness of the pain of guilt, and a willingness to mediate the healing and redeeming love of God. When the pastor is most truly the pastor as his people have learned to see him, he can be the instrument to serve an end that is nowhere served in quite the same way by the professional counselor. This does not mean that the pastor skilled in counseling techniques and rich in psychological understanding cannot employ all that he has learned with benefit. However, he does it within a setting that is unique in our society, both from the point of view of what he is and, equally important, from the point of view of what his people think he is. The ability to function within such a doubly envisaged role demands an unusual degree of psychological skill, for it implies that the pastor must take people as they are and where he finds them. He cannot retreat to the safe confines of a carefully structured relationship. The pastor is a shepherd. He not only feeds a flock, he also goes after those that stray. But he goes not to condemn or to return to a judging community. Rather, out of a loving concern, he seeks to restore the lost sheep, or the sheep with problems, to the sustaining structure of right relations.

So the pastoral call is now, as always, an opportunity that is unique in the approach to people. It must change with the changing demands of the parish and the changing skills of the pastor. But as long as men and women have special needs, and can be reached by those specially endowed to meet the needs, the pastor's privileged approach to people is sacred.

14

PASTORAL CARE THROUGH
PREACHING

PREACHING can also be a pastoral function. The sheep hear his voice and they follow him because they know him. The pastor who lives close to his people, knows their lives, and shares their fortunes, is not separated from his people when he enters the pulpit on a Sunday morning. He stands as one who is their pastor, and they listen because he is part of the spiritual dimension of their living.

The process by which the preacher comes to know his people is no simple one. It involves a careful study of people in general, the way they develop, the things that interfere with their growth, the morbid states of mind and emotion that may possess them, and the common aspirations that motivate them. He seeks to know people, great and small. The great ones he can study through their biographies and the contributions they have made to life and history. The small ones he can know through visiting in their homes, sharing their times of joy and sadness, sensing their feelings when they cannot express them, and accepting them when they are perhaps expressed too well.

The serious student of pastoral preaching will also study people in depth. Here his pastoral counseling will help him to sense those inner reaches of being that are usually shielded from the outside world. Here his intensive study of personality development and regression, the normal and the abnormal, will enrich his insight. Careful reading of case studies will deepen his understanding of the things that happen to people. He will study the social forces in which his people are enmeshed, and will be aware of the problems of employment that engage their lives. Nothing that happens to his people will be foreign to him.

He will also try to know what his people read, how they use their leisure time, and what engages their interest in the community. He will be interested in the school play, the chorus concert, and the athletic events of the community, not because this is his pastime, but because it is his occupation to be aware of what is happening to his people so that he may more effectively relate his message to their experience.

His message is one of life. He does not talk about life as much as he talks about the life that they experience. Just as Jesus used the common everyday events as a point of reference for his message, so the pastoral preacher should never present a message that is unrelated to his people and their existence.

When he enters the pulpit on Sunday he relates to his people but he is always careful not to expose them. Any knowledge that he has of individuals, and any information that is privileged must never leak into a sermon, even by indirection. It is hazardous even to say "Someone came to me recently," for any who have come are apprehensive lest their confidential revelations may be held up as an example for others. In any human situation there is a biblical counterpart, and the insight may be just as penetrating though its source is centuries away in time and thousands of miles away in space.

When the pastor opens his mouth to speak, he speaks to his people about their lives, their needs and their problems. He does it not in a way that adds anxiety to what already disturbs them; rather he speaks of the value of their life in the sight of God. He emphasizes their endowment as children of God. He affirms their faith and in so doing enhances it. He speaks of their power to become more than they are. He does not chastise them for their failure; he helps them to see that failure is not necessary, that they can find within themselves the resources they need for each day of life. As he emphasizes the value of life they become more valuable in their own eyes, and the effort to achieve a better way of life is justified. Because he believes deeply in the value of his message, he communicates it to them not only by what he says but also by what he is.

The pastoral preacher is always aware that his message is three dimensional. He does not speak to the conscious mind alone, but uses symbols rich in meaning to set the deeper levels of being to work. Because he shares a long tradition of pulpit utterance, he is not alone when he speaks. He is always surrounded by a cloud of witnesses, some of whom he would be glad to associate with and others whose influence he decries. But they are there, and when his people come to church to hear him, they unconsciously listen to the other voices who to them represent the preaching ministry. Yet even while he is aware of the symbols that work at the lower levels of consciousness, he seeks to open the channels of communication to make his people responsive to the Holy Spirit.

The pastor in the pulpit is also aware that his message is given a special setting by tradition. It is a part of a service of worship. It is unique among types of public utterance, for the person who speaks and his purpose in speaking are accepted as being in the public interest, for the good of humanity. This status is protected by law; no minister can be prosecuted under the libel laws for a statement made in a sermon. His sermon is granted immunity because of its recognized function as an instrument of public morals. It is assumed that what is said in a sermon is for the good of man. This places an obligation on the preacher to be sure that what he says *is* for the good of mankind.

The disciplines that have developed around the counseling ministry raise questions about the preaching function. How much of what is said from the pulpit is a projection of disordered emotions in the preacher? How often is the pulpit used as a means of aggressive action? How often is what is said from the pulpit a violation of sound counseling practice? Does the pulpit have privileges that are denied in the counseling room? If so, what are they and why are they granted?

It may be assumed that pastoral preaching growing out of a clear understanding of counseling diciplines and restraints will carry these insights into pulpit utterance, without violating the approach to persons, and yet recognizing that the purpose of the sermon is broader than the process of the counseling room. A sermon is an affirmation of faith, an interpretation of biblical truth, as well as a source of inspiration. Affirming one's faith that the personality will seek its best expression is implicit in the counseling room but explicit in the sermon. The interpretation of biblical truth may be incidental to the counseling process, but it is essential in the sermon. The source of inspiration in the counseling room is personal and indirect, but in the sermon it is central in thought and structural in utterance.

Both the counseling process and the sermon are interested in motivating change. In the counseling room the pace is set by the counselee, and the emphasis is on the inner resources of the counselee. The sermon deliberately seeks to bring about changes in thinking and action by creating interest and winning loyalty to a Christian way of life. The preacher makes no apologies for what he tries to do, for this is the underlying purpose of preaching. But when he engages in the study of human personality and the disciplines of counseling, he approaches his pulpit task with a chastened spirit, for he knows that many of the things that have been done traditionally to motivate change have been unwarranted, superficial, and in some instances damaging. While he still wants to motivate change, he is willing to recognize that human growth and the process of becoming is not dictated from without, but is rather stimulated from within. To that end he holds up an ideal toward which people may grow. He indicates the broad outlines of a way of life, knowing that each individual must adapt the message to his individual needs.

The sermon becomes then an opportunity to help people see themselves in a mirror, to judge whether or not they are measuring up to an ideal. The efforts to interpret the ideal revealed in the life of Christ may be presented in a way that emphasizes possibilities for personal application. The change then is motivated by desire rather than by threats.

The mood of the sermon is one of quiet contemplation, so that the individual, in the quiet depths of his own being, gains a perspective that is real for him. In the atmosphere of worship, the person may be alone with his deepest thoughts and at the same time aware of a tradition, a way of life, and a group of people sharing a common quest for meaning. When people comment that the preacher was speaking directly to them, they do not mean that they felt singled out or exposed, but rather that they were stimulated to think about their own behavior, their way of life, and their personal needs.

The sermon holds up an ideal and seeks to motivate change but it also tries to furnish the motive power for that change. It seeks to infuse life into the ideal so that the hearer wants to become what he realizes he can become. Sometimes people come to a pastor for counseling after a period of secular therapy saying something like this: "I have gained insight into my problem and I understand the source of it. I have adjusted myself to some of the circumstances of life, but the goal seems out of reach. I do not have the inner strength to achieve it." Here is where inspiration becomes important, for it can become the energizing force to stimulate the person to become what he wants to become.

So the pastoral preacher senses the importance of inspiration as essential to achievement. He holds up an ideal, but he also tries to make it seem important for the individual and worth the effort to make it true for him. Sometimes the process may be as simple as showing that others have done it, and you can too. At other times it may be a more subtle firing of the spirit with an awareness of its power. This can be done by an appeal to move beyond the plateaus of easy self-acceptance in order to face an as yet unrealized self. It may dramatize the satisfactions of personal achievement. It may single out the nature of the highest self by making the mind of Christ a living fact. It may appeal to the emotions by making the spirit of Christ real enough to become a basis for personal action. It may inspire the efforts to try to do the good a person understands but fails to practice. The processes of inspiration appeal not so much to the mind as to the deeper emotional needs that implement knowledge through action. For the act of being a better person is not so much a matter of knowledge as it is a matter of determined effort. Inspiration helps to make a person feel that the effort is warranted.

One does not set the soul ablaze with purpose by a series of unrelated abstractions. The pastor who approaches his pulpit task each week with the question, "What shall I preach?" is not apt to speak directly to his people. Instead his approach must be, "To whom will I be speaking and what are their needs?" With that question in mind, his acts of preparation begin with a quiet look at the people who will sit before him. He tries to sense their feelings and the varied needs that bring them together on a Sunday morning. He tries to move into their thoughts and feelings so that he is at one with them. Then, having established clearly in his own mind the persons to whom he will be speaking, he moves on to consider how best he may use his resources of understanding, training in biblical interpretation, and awareness of personal needs to create something that speaks directly to those needs.

All that he has learned from the art of counseling will then come to his aid in sermon preparation. He will start where his people are, move with them, and help them to move with him. He will realize that his preaching has the quality of a personal encounter. In one sense he will not be speaking to them but will be speaking for them. He will gather up their aspirations and give them an expression. This will make it possible for them to say to themselves, this is what I believe, this is what I feel, and this is what

I want for my life. From the first sentence, he will speak their thoughts. In contrast to the counseling room, where he may speak their thoughts after them, to give them a chance to see how they sound, he will hold up thoughts they do not yet have the insight to phrase, though the desire may be there. From the first sentence, he will build with logic and persuasion a structure of meaning to make life look more worth the living, not merely an empty round of days. The meaning will be a challenge to the best that is within them. They will see themselves in a new light, for the light of God's purposes and meaning for their lives will be thrown upon the events of the days. Then parents will interpret their problems with their children not with a concern for their own frustation but with an interest in the valued souls that are emerging through this difficult behavior. The employer will see his employees as people with aspirations and lives of their own, with problems and privileges over and above the time and talent he has bought on the labor market. People who have trouble keeping their feelings within proper bounds will see themselves not as hopeless pawns of their own impulses, but as creatures with the power of self-mastery. The encounter of mind with mind, and feeling with feeling, will bear fruit in proportion to its real interest in real persons. In this light a sermon becomes more than a homiletic exercise. It becomes an experience of communication in depth, where soul speaks to soul, and answers come in the determination to live more wisely and well with the help of God.

The pastor who is close to his people during the week will find it easier to be close to them in the act of preaching.

The pastor who shares the deep feelings of his people through the counseling process will find that he can construct of his experience an understanding of need that will bolster his preaching efforts. His sermons will then take on a quality of expression, marked by sympathy and sensitivity, to which his people will respond. His life will become the richer for it, for the demands for a creative venture in the pulpit each week will not be an exercise in futility, but in speaking the words of life. His preaching with pastoral interest will then become another dimension of a total ministry. It will bridge the gap between pulpit and pew, and will make it easier for his people to come to him for personal counseling in their times of need. They will sense that he understands their needs and is not far off.

15

WHEN THE PASTOR
MUST BE THE PROPHET

THERE are times when the pastor must speak the word of truth with courage. At first glance it may appear that this compromises his role as pastor, for how can the loving shepherd chastise his sheep? It may not be a pleasant task, but when the course of events clearly portends disaster, the pastor cannot afford the luxury of remaining quiet. A pastoral role that deprives the ministry of its right to make the prophetic utterance demands more of a man than is warranted. Part of the task of spiritual leadership is the obligation to hold up human circumstances so that they may be clearly seen for all of their destructiveness. When such times come the pastor cannot wisely compromise his mission by unhealthy silence.

The pastor's concern for people does not begin or end with his efforts to help them find a personal way of life that can ease them through their problems. Part of man's problem grows from the struggle to find moral meaning in a society that places immoral demands upon him. When the pastor sees a clear and present danger in the encroachments of society upon the lives of his people, he must speak. By speaking he does not deny a pastoral concern; rather he projects it into the larger circle of events that shape life, sometimes with subtlety and sometimes with cataclysmic force.

We are surrounded with secular prophets. We are urged constantly to invest wisely with the aid of those who foresee market trends. We listen each morning to those who prophesy what the weather will be, and approach our holidays with the advantage of an extended weather forecast. It is not unreasonable for those who are concerned with man's moral and spiritual welfare to look at the present with an eye to the future.

The prophetic ministry has three characteristics: to foresee, to foretell, and to forestall.

To foresee, the prophet needs the depth perception that

a study of history gives. While this insight into history is rooted in economic and social forces, it does not get far away from the effect of these forces on people. It knows enough of the past to interpret the present and weigh the meanings of present action. It knows, for instance, that arms races invariably lead to arms use. It knows that on the basis of historic precedent, psychotic traffic in weapons leads to the insanity of trigger-pulling. It knows that economic injustice leads to violent action in order to right the wrongs. It knows that racial inequalities lead to damaged persons, both among those who suffer the injustice and those who perpetrate it.

This ability to preview the future on the basis of the past has scriptural precedent. The great preachers of the Old Testament viewed the hazards of the ways of life of the Jewish people. The prophets were the political analysts of their day, but they spoke not out of concern for secular progress but rather from their belief that the judgments of time were the judgments of God. They felt that God was not separated from the group life of men, and that a violation of the will of God produced inevitable consequences for the guilty people.

The role of the prophet was not only to foresee but to foretell. So the prophet was an ingenious communicator. His conviction was so clearly defined that he was willing to invest it with cosmic authority. His "Thus saith the Lord" gave the ring of authority to his best insight, and his skill in persuasion and his power of logic gave force to his ideas. It is not strange that the great prophets were also powerful preachers. They had the courage to face the people with unpopular truths, to predict consequences, and to suffer the rejection that often accompanies undesired insight. With the skill that grows from understanding people, the prophets used varied ways in trying to present their message winsomely. God's judgment of social evil compelled Amos's warnings; the herdsman's skill in presenting his ideas made the judgments cumulative with the experience of his neighbors, so that they could not easily fail to see themselves in the same light. Hosea tied the pathos of personal tragedy to the social collapse that came with unfaithfulness to God. Isaiah used the rich poetry so cherished in Jewish tradition as the vehicle to communicate his vision of impending tragedy. Invariably the prophet was a man of courage who spoke the painful truth with clarity and power.

We miss the main purpose of prophetic utterance if we see it as merely designed to foretell. The prophet was concerned with social salvation. He wanted to save people and groups from the tragic consequences of the actions he saw and warned about. Even in tragic circumstances he tried to point out that it was not too late to return to the Lord. Isaiah called upon men to mend their ways, cease their evil, and learn the good. Jeremiah pleaded for the devout life as the way of overcoming the ways of iniquity. Even in exile or social catastrophe, men can learn the ways of God and be restored to right relationships *within,* pending the restoration of right relations *without.* In fact, the wise management of the inner kingdom helps to create conditions for reform and restitution in the external circumstances of life. In dealing with motives and means of social change the prophet never became so engrossed in sociological considerations or economic forces that he lost sight of the power of the person as the instrument for effecting change.

Often the prophet possessed a psychic sense that made it possible for him to be aware of those truths that were not easily accessible to ordinary men. But even this extra-sensory capacity was always measured by the nature of God and history, and the false prophets were separated from the true prophets by the fruits of their judgment as well as by the accuracy of their interpretation of history and their deep concern for the welfare of the people.

The struggle of Jesus with false religion and political corruption is a major theme of the New Testament. From the time he first preached, he challenged the selfish and false assumptions of those who heard him. In the end he was tried on false charges so that his judgments of the religious and political leaders of his time might be quieted. It is significant that among the varied subjects of the beatitudes only one subject was worthy of two beatitudes, and that concerned the suffering and reward of those who were persecuted for righteousness' sake.

St. Paul was always in trouble with political and economic forces in his day because he put people before profits, and truth before the behavior of the unscrupulous. The disciples went about the tasks of turning the world upside down not because they were trouble-makers, but because they possessed a new understanding of the relationships between man and God, and saw it challenged about them on every side.

St. Francis was overwhelmed by the plight of the common people, and he started a movement within the Church to try to meet these needs. His movement was taken over and destroyed from within by those who felt that his concern threatened the social and economic advantage they had gained by ignoring such needs.

Savonarola spoke vigorously against the social abuses of his day, and for his prophetic utterance suffered the fate of the prophet. It was no accident that Martin Luther became involved in theological controversy at the point where he challenged economic abuse in the name of religion. John Wesley proclaimed the value of the individual in the midst of a calloused economic system that considered people cheap and machines valuable.

The religious impulse has always been closely associated with the prophet's voice. When the forces that damage human personality are taken for what they are, destroyers of the raw material of God's kingdom, the prophet's voice will be heard.

But it is not easy to be a prophet. Many people have been aware of the destructive forces in society, but few have lifted their voices in opposition. A gospel concerned only with patching up damage done by social injustice is only half a gospel. A ministry concerned only with the achievement of personal adjustment in the midst of the forces that demand new and better adjustments is concentrating on effects rather than causes.

The pastor who is genuinely concerned with the welfare of his people is bound to have an interest in whatever forces cripple or destroy their spirits. To let a child play with poisonous snakes, with the assurance that a snake bite serum is available, is neither good logic nor considerate of the child. Something better can be done.

THE PASTOR MUST BE THE PROPHET

The values of a social order that are continuously under-
mining the religious and social values of the individual must
be challenged in the name of religious integrity. To pray
for God's kingdom to come among men, and then give all
our attention to binding up the wounds of those injured
by a corrupt social order, is but a part of the task. We must
give integrity to our prayers by seeking a social order that
fulfills the needs of men instead of expecting them to
achieve the good life in spite of what surrounds them.

There are times when mere adjustments to the destructive forces in life is not only inadequate, but a compromise
with that destruction. I stood once with the father of a
young woman who had died a horrible death of radium
poisoning contracted in a clock factory where she painted
dials on clocks. It was important to bring the consoling
insights of the Christian message to this bereaved parent,
but to treat the effect and ignore the cause would have been
only part of the pastoral obligation. It was also important
to work for the program of the labor organization which
demanded that safeguards be developed so that such a
needless death might not occur again.

To engage in a pastoral ministry that helps people to
learn techinques of relaxation, so that they may better meet
the stress of life, is only part of the task if these people are
sent out into a world where competition is the law of life
and men's efforts to outwit and out-pressure each other are
the cause of the stress. To use the rich resources of the
Christian faith merely to seek inner peace is a denial of a
major part of the ministry.

It has been observed that where a pastor is close to his
people, and has established beyond any doubt his genuine

interest in their welfare, he is granted a freedom to express his convictions and work toward those goals that are within the scope of the prophetic ministry. Because he is trusted in his relationship with people, he is also trusted in regard to social reform. While his people may not always agree with him and may even actively oppose him, they do not try to destroy him. They believe in him as a person. Some of the most courageous prophetic voices of our day come from pulpits where the right of the pastor to speak is guaranteed by the worth of his pastoral ministry. Some erratic and disturbing voices that wear the cloak of the prophet are challenged and rejected because the speakers have failed to establish in the minds of their hearers any real interest in people. The minister who is always in trouble with his congregation over social issues is apt to be one who has no effective relationship with his people. They reject him because, for reasons that seem apparent to them, he has first rejected them. The shepherd who ignores his sheep, or is an absentee leader, will find it hard to convince them that his voice is the true voice.

The pastoral ministry may be an escape from some of the unpleasant aspects of the total ministry. The pastor who spends more and more time with fewer and fewer people is undoubtedly ignoring or neglecting some phases of his parish work. The pastor who becomes absorbed in more and more detailed liturgical procedures often employs this interest to get away from people and their problems. Also, the minister who wants to be primarily the prophet and lead endless crusades may be using this method of escape from the essential pastoral role.

THE PASTOR MUST BE THE PROPHET

There is a point at which the pastoral ministry and the prophetic concern are two sides of the same coin, and support and supplement each other in their expression. Although the prophet may still pay some penalties for his prophesying, the toll will not be so heavy if he first wins the support of his people by a sound and effective pastoral ministry. His people will be more apt to accept his prophetic insights if they are aware of his insights into the total role of the pastor.

A recent event supports this contention. A pastor—who for years had carried out a pastoral ministry close to his people and their needs—championed an unpopular cause in the community. He was labeled as subversive by some who could think of no valid arguments against his position. Determined to destroy him and his influence in the community, they printed a leaflet intended to show that he had a long record of association with questionable causes. It was a clever example of "guilt by association." This was sent at the expense of the group, which seemed to have plenty of money, to everyone whose phone was listed in the local telephone directory. But this didn't create the expected reaction in the congregation; a committee called on the pastor to see what it could do to ease his mind. Another group met to take action against those who had distributed the leaflet. To both groups the pastor expressed his appreciation for support, but said he felt the less said the better, and the matter was forgotten in no time. He attributed this healthy community response to an effective pastoral ministry.

The pastor must sometimes be a prophet and speak his

mind with courage and conviction. But he can do it best when he has laid a firm foundation of pastoral concern for his people. Then they will support his right to speak as he sees fit and many of them will come to share the prophet's concern.

16

SOCIAL DIMENSIONS OF A PASTORAL MINISTRY

*I*N THE previous chapter we considered the philosophical and theoretical aspects of a social ministry as inseparably bound up with the awareness of the needs of people. In this chapter we direct our attention more specifically to the social problems of our day that impinge upon the lives of our people, and what may be done to direct effective effort toward relieving them.

A psychiatrist once justified to me his deep concern for social change by saying, "What sense does it make to patch up persons and then send them back into the same social forces that broke them in the first place?" Perhaps the question is over-simplified, but it does warrant consideration as we mull over those conditions in society that damage or destroy a person's ability to function satisfactorily.

Each individual is related to a variety of institutions and social forces. The school, the church, the place of employment, the places of recreation, and the political structure affect his life just as he in someway shapes the institutions of which he is a part. The formal institutions are continually being influenced by informal forces: prejudices, social fears, and group impulses. The individual is often caught in forces he does not understand and cannot control. These may frustrate the goals of his life, sometimes producing in him an impotence that reduces him to a level of brutishness. I have seen people in the aftermath of war so reduced in spiritual stature that their goals were gone and their hopes were shattered. In a meaningless round of days they struggled to gain the mere substance to preserve biological life, for there seemed to be little else to which they could fruitfully direct their energies. They were pawns in the struggles of men and nations, reduced to valuelessness.

A few centuries before Christ, Plato tried to define the bounds and purposes of man's social existence in The Republic. He sought a social structure that could fulfill the highest aims of group life and at the same time use the resources of the individual fruitfully. But in his structure he granted freedom to people like himself at the expense of those who worked to support his goals. His plan established the benevolent dictatorship of the intellectual.

In more recent years the pattern of communism has sought to use the power of an industrial era to guarantee the fair fruits of that power for the workers who manned the machines. The intellectuals worked for the state to improve the machinery, and the artists worked to enrich the lives of the people, but all were bound by the ruthless dictatorship of the proletariat which exercised power through the political party. Freedom was limited by the dictates of the state, and the individual and his rights were secondary to the state's interests.

St. Augustine, a few centuries after Christ, wrote of the City of God, concerned with the fulfillment of the innate destinies of men as being worthy of the good life, protected by social forces equally concerned with that good. The basic philosophy was in part incorporated in the structure of the Roman Catholic Church as the divinely appointed institution concerned with the welfare of men's souls. But here again, with time the institution became the end, and the men the means toward that end.

The democratic idea emerged with men's need to exercise economic freedom in order to exploit natural resources and gain the benefits of industrialization. Freedom to develop resources became in many instances a freedom to exploit, and the morals of capitalism became enmeshed with the processes of democracy. Yet the demands of freedom supplied an inner corrective process that has given to democratic development a capacity for change. The blind spots of democracy are the blind spots of humanity. Many of the founding fathers who claimed that all men are created equal did not relate this to the human slaves they owned. When claims of freedom were made, they did not always support the right of workers to protect their labor, or the right of minority groups to express their ways of life and thought. But the democratic process keeps injustice from becoming entrenched and guarantees the right of peaceful change when the pressures become intolerable.

The Protestant tradition is related to the democratic tradition by common needs and historical accident. Because it has always had a place in the common development, it still works for changes it feels will create a social climate wherein all men can fulfill their destinies. More than we realize, this has granted to the church a place of leadership in social thought, and has placed upon the church an obligation to be socially sensitive.

The pastor in any community is in a position to sense social and racial and economic injustice. He is morally obligated to use the resources of spiritual leadership to make men aware of their value, and to upgrade the processes by which democracy works out its ways of dealing with people and their needs. The pastor who takes a part in the processes of social change is well within the democratic tradition, for democracy at its best is built on the value of man and his right to act individually and collectively for what he believes is right.

The pastor can express his concern for people at the point where they make their living. In industrial communities he can help shape opinion as to what are fair labor practices. In one community the manager of the largest industry and the president of the labor council were members of the same church and active in the same church men's club. When a serious labor conflict developed, the labor union went on strike, but, by arrangement with the plant management, continued to work. The strike was in name only. The negotiations were carried on informally in the pastor's study with a primary concern for human values and fair dealing all round. The church, as an instrument of group reconciliation, was well within the historic tradition when it used its influence to help men understand each other's problems and arrive at a non-violent and mutually respectful agreement. Often anger and destructive emotions accumulate until it is difficult for the real issues to be kept clearly in focus. The pastor may be the symbol of, and the instrument for, achieving right relations.

For many of his people the major social problem is the possibility of war. Young people find it difficult to make their plans for the future without taking into account their prospects of military service. Parents fear lest their children suffer the consequences of military action. The prospects of atomic fallout, with its consequences for health, is a constant source of uneasiness. The idea of fallout shelters fills many people with apprehension because they feel there is no real protection against nuclear annihilation. At the same time they feel helpless to do anything constructive about the problem. Serious differences of opinion exist and most people feel that they do not have adequate information about the real state of affairs.

So the prospects of war, with the many problems that

cluster about it, are a persistent source of anxiety. In any state of anxiety the inability to do anything constructive compounds the feelings. The church has an important stake in maintaining a world of peace. Disintegration of morals, family life, and retardation of social progress always accompany war, not to speak of the endless destruction of human life and property. The church cannot ignore problems of this stature. The teachings of the New Testament are explicit. The concern of the Christian tradition is to create understanding of the problems that lead to war, and to create the goodwill that can help to eliminate it.

There are many things that can be done to foster and increase understanding. The mission program of the church gives people a chance to invest in constructive international relations. The use of the democratic process to influence the thinking of government officials is not to be ignored. The active support of movements that can create goodwill is to be encouraged. Spreading information about the futility of nuclear conflict may well deter an unbridled trust in weapons as a means of safety. In all of the ways open to him, the pastor can help to keep his people alert to those constructive acts they can perform, in order to contribute to a body of sentiment that cannot easily be ignored. The state of helpless submission is a poor substitute for constructive action, wherever it may be taken. Sometimes the efforts seem futile, but the alternatives leave no choice but to use every opportunity to oppose the forces that move toward irreparable destruction.

A major social problem calling for pastoral leadership concerns race. Nowhere is the democratic process more in jeopardy, and the basic conviction of the Christian tradition more openly violated, than in the matters of racial practice. To judge a person because of something for which he is not responsible threatens the inner state of the discriminator more than it does the external state of those discriminated against. Usually the emotional condition of the prejudiced person is so extreme that logic cannot easily bridge it. A "conditioning experience" to set in motion new feelings is needed, since prejudice is basically a matter of insecurity. The apprehensions that go with prejudice are so deep-rooted that they take precedence over religious convictions and common courtsey. The disease of the emotions is so deep-rooted that the simplest observations are ignored.

The Christian fellowship should accept people on the basis of their Christian character and interest. To that end the church should be an institution that values people without regard to external characteristics or appearances. When the church begins to practice this type of acceptance, the other institutions of society will catch the flavor of this acceptance. Yet too often the church lags behind the practice and precedent of other institutions. If the pastor sets the pace in his preaching and in his practice, others can take courage and begin to practice what they know in their minds but deny in their emotions.

A subtle force that affects thinking is the dominant secular mood of our culture. The impact of the scientific attitude reaches deeply into the beliefs of people. They may continue to give lip service to traditional religion, but in practice their thinking is dominated by what science says. Applied science has changed the world in a few decades, while the preachments of religion have made no comparable impression. When people compare the results, they feel inclined to give science the influential place in their thinking. Theoretical science has made its deep impression on the concept of man and his place in the nature of things. The Copernican revolution removed the earth from the center of creation. The Darwinian revolution took man out of his position as a special creation and related him to all the rest of life. The Freudian revolution told man his mind was not what he thought it was, the final arbiter of his destiny, but that the sources of his motivation are more complex and often beyond the reach of rational processes. The revolution of Einstein tells man that matter is not what he thought it was, but that the things that seem real are actually bundles of energy too minute to be sensed by the crude equipment man uses to understand the outside world.

And now yet another revolution is turning men's minds away from the earth toward interstellar space, with the prospect of exploration and colonization on other solar bodies. In each instance the reaction of traditional religion has been to oppose the new insights of science, and only after delay and overpowering necessity to make an uneasy peace with new scientific truth. People may wonder if religious insight is always wrong and slow to be convinced. The pastor who contends with the secular mind must be aware of what is happening in the world of science, for though the first impression supports the secular thesis, the upper-level scientist is essentially a mystic, dealing with forces he will never see, recognizing a basic unity in all that exists, and responsive to inspirations that challenge his spirit in a way that is akin to a true religious consciousness. Science works within a limited set of principles, and while some discoveries tend to discount religious ideas, they are also a stimulus to the religious consciousness to grow, for no religious insight is adequate that cannot make room for any truth. The pastor who helps shape the thinking of young people intrigued by scientific discovery must be alert to what science has to say. He must also be willing to explore these important areas of human experience beyond the scope of scientific inquiry. Here problems can be resolved by achieving a higher synthesis of thought. For science can furnish the equipment to make a better world, but it takes better men to know how to use it creatively.

The complex world in which we live is continually having its impact on the thoughts and feelings of those whom we serve as pastors. The achieving of right understanding and right relations within the self, and among men and groups and nations, does not come about by ignoring the difficult problems yet to be solved. The pastoral ministry must be continually at work, raising questions that may not have been considered, holding up ideals not yet achieved, and stimulating those types of understanding that can build bridges between men where walls once were.

We started this book with a plea for a theology that was concerned with the development of right relations within the self, with other men, and with cosmic reality. We have tried through these pages to point out some of the ways in which the pastoral ministry can perform this important task. In conclusion, we point out that the pastoral ministry does not complete its work until it takes seriously the role of the Christian in the structure of society. It is here that any personal wholeness that is developed has a chance to verify itself by building a social order within which men may dwell in understanding and goodwill.

The pastoral ministry is no simple task. It invites the best training and the most skilled practice to help people live with wisdom in our complicated society. It calls for the best there is in a man. It calls, in fact, for all there is of him. Without the mind of Christ we cannot understand the will of God for life, and without the spirit of Christ we cannot find the motive power to achieve it. And without both we cannot build the living body of Christ in the life of a church that is to know his will and do it. The pastor is ordained for this work, and that ordination calls for an ever-larger vision of the task he has requested and which opportunity has handed him.